IN ROADS

A Working Solution to America's War on Drugs

CHARLES HAINES

authorHOUSE®

AuthorHouse™
1663 Liberty Drive
Bloomington, IN 47403
www.authorhouse.com
Phone: 1-800-839-8640

First published by AuthorHouse   11/30/2011

ISBN: 978-1-4685-0874-1 (sc)
ISBN: 978-1-4685-0875-8 (ebk)

Library of Congress Control Number: 2011961749

Printed in the United States of America

Any people depicted in stock imagery provided by
Thinkstock are models, and such images are being used
for illustrative purposes only.
Certain stock imagery © Thinkstock.

This book is printed on acid-free paper.

TABLE OF CONTENTS

"Slay your dragon,
but don't let the slaying of your dragon
make you a dragon, too."

-Brad Zentmyer

Acknowledgement

The inspiration for writing this compilation was not hard to gain from studying the lives of Joe David, Mike Lewis, and Robbie Bishop. Without these men and the paths they carved, our world would be a terrible place.

Joe David, it was a true honor to sit across the table from you and not only gather your information, but also sense your incredible passion for this cause. I deeply thank you for your participation.

Mike Lewis, your drive and devotion is second to none and your intensity could inspire the most timid of souls. I am gracious for all of your assistance.

Lisa Bishop-Webb and Justin Webb, despite not working the streets everyday with us, your everlasting dedication and support of our cause will always be a driving force. Without your help, Robbie's legacy would have been impossible to capture. I am forever indebted.

To Mason and Ashlyn, who are the best children a father could ever ask for and are my constant motivation to effect positive change in the world.

And to my wife, Amy, who has always shown me unconditional support and given me the confidence to keep improving myself and crusade for what is right.

PREFACE

In December of 2003, 17 year old Robert Rehm left the home of a friend to begin the short walk to his grandmother's house where he was staying while his mother was serving with the US military in Iraq. Robert was only three days away from flying to a Christmas reunion with her in Germany.

Robert's path to Grandma's took him through the turf of a notorious street gang that was responsible for frequent and bold shootings in a suburban community that was firmly in their grasp. For almost a decade, this criminal organization controlled a majority of the drug enterprise in the city. Chances were, if you were looking to buy cocaine or marijuana in this town, it would be supplied by these kings of the street corner; and they were hell-bent on ensuring that no one ever thought about interfering with their monopoly.

Just a few steps from his buddy's house, Robert's body was riddled by a hail bullets fired by two assassins, on patrol for rival gang members. Robert was left lying cold and lifeless, until a nearby resident noticed the body and phoned police a short time later.

Robert would be one of many cases of mistaken identity. He was not a gang member or drug pusher.

He was not deliberately treading on their turf or showing these men any disrespect. However, when it came to ensuring black market profit at the cost of another's life, these criminals were careless and remorseless, intended target or not.

Christmas season, four years later, 17 year old Michael York tagged along with some high school friends to a house party located in a modest suburban Chicago neighborhood. Michael would not leave the house alive. The demise of this young son and brother would not be a drunken driving crash or freak accident. It would be at the point of a heroin needle.

Going with the flow of a good time and the subversion of his peers, Michael injected the poison into his vein, in search of the infamous rush brought on by this venom. As his body lay back, resonating from the toxic influx, Michael slipped from consciousness. By morning, his young heart had shut down. He rested cold and lifeless, in an unfamiliar house, to be discovered by the same people he called friends the night before. Those "friends" would quickly abandon any allegiance to his life, for the sake of their own.

Hours later, Michael's body was insensitively dumped in a cold, snow-covered alley way in Chicago, during his associates' next drug run to the city to fulfill their insatiable addiction. Michael became just another statistic in the tragedy of youth heroin abuse.

Circa 2009, as markets crashed and job layoffs spread at an alarming pace, local governments were crippled by a lack of funding from the usual tax sources. The phasing-out of important community programs and services was inevitable, and the traditional security of government and civil service employment became uncertain.

Cities, large and small, began announcing million dollar budget deficits, along with their plans to hand out pink slips to vital public servants and raise taxes on citizens who were experiencing the financial grips of a strong recession. It seemed as though government was in serious threat of financial ruin, with few alternatives for restructuring their operational cash flow.

Tragic stories of young lives stopped short, and cases of financial hardship can be read in newspapers covering communities of all sizes throughout our nation. The topics are so frequent that the emotional effects on the reader sometimes fade from desensitization. However, these are our youth and the future of our country. Their loss is not acceptable, and there are viable means to deter the causes of their deaths.

Unemployment and declining government services in this economy are daunting concerns that are frequently voiced. Local governments struggle to make ends meet and search to find progressive and viable sources of income without traditional and substantial tax increases.

Drugs, death, crime, and financial ruin are very real concerns in our society. The sporadic crusades against narcotics, lead by law enforcement, have become cliché. We, as a nation, have even considered throwing in the towel, or at least decriminalizing certain drugs in effort to focus our resources on "more important crime."

However, what if there was a two pronged approach to rectifying the issues that grip our nation on a daily basis? What if this strategy was well established and had astounding results within the very few communities that have successfully employed this method?

While there have been many publications that speak to the importance of America's "War on Drugs," not many writings have exposed a pragmatic solution . . . a solution that can save thousands of young lives lost to drug-related violence, and alleviate our governments' suppressive financial burden.

I have worked as a police officer since 1998, and I have been involved in some facet of law enforcement since 1994. As a rookie patrol deputy for a Sheriff's Office just outside of Chicago, Illinois, I quickly fell in love with the cat-and-mouse game of drug detection.

My passion for this issue is derived from my first-hand involvement in my own corner of the world. The cases of Robert Rehm and Michael York are troubling examples of violent criminal and drug activity from my home town. Keeping the community safe in which I was born and raised is a cause that is close to my heart as I take to the streets every day.

While "cutting my teeth" in drug detection, it was always quite a rush to seek out and pull over local drug dealers and users, then find means to conduct a lawful search of them and their vehicles while dealing with their usual belligerence and disrespect for "the law."

Ultimately, the payoff would come when they would break down during the discovery of whatever dope they decided to stash in some inconspicuous location within their car.

After experiencing drug detection success in a uniform, I was assigned to a narcotics investigation group early in my career. In that capacity, I began seeing the direct effects on neighborhood crime rates as we plucked street dealers out of the communities. If we targeted the dope dealers of a given area in our county where we saw an increase in gang activity or burglaries, the number of those crimes would dramatically decrease or cease altogether . . . for a month or two . . . until someone else took over.

When I transferred to a nearby sheriff's department, and returned to the assignment of a uniformed patrolman, it became even more evident to me that focused drug enforcement had a substantial impact on the local crime rate. At the time, gang activity was extremely high in one specific community. The city would experience a shooting victim at least weekly and typically one specific gang was the perpetrator of the senseless rampage. This street gang was financially and socially supported by street-level drug trafficking, as most are. Besides random shootings, the associated criminal activity in the form of burglaries, robberies, etc were also very high.

From the zealous position of a young cop, I reveled in the challenge of the prevalence of this subculture by making quite a few substantial drug arrests. The policing opportunities supported by this criminal society became a firm launching pad for my career.

Two years after I started at this new agency, a federally-lead investigation resulted in the indictment and apprehension of over twenty prominent members of the gang. Immediately thereafter, it seemed criminal activity fell off a ledge. There were rarely gang fights, shootings, or killings. By way of comparison, at the height of the gang's stronghold in 2005, there were 14 murders reported in the suburban town; by 2008, only 2 homicides manifested in the same area[i].

The associated crime dropped off, as well, and the police agency, was not responding to the same volume of reports of vandalized property, stolen cars, shootings or murders. The availability of drugs also seemed slimmer, as evidenced by the users I encountered, who were reporting the lack of illicit substances on the streets.

The large-scale investigation was exhaustive and utilized hundreds of officers from several local, state, and federal jurisdictions, over the span of almost a year, to secure and execute the multitude of search and arrest warrants that brought the case to a close.

However weakened, factions of the same gang (and others) began rebuilding in the area. Complaints of low drug availability and high costs faded, and I found myself responding to more and more property crime reports. It seemed the town was back on track as a notorious crime culture and drug source.

During the same time frame, I was tasked with handling a drug detection dog. The opportunity of being a narcotics canine handler was incredibly exciting to me, mostly because it would facilitate more anti-drug work.

One afternoon shift, I was listening to a fellow deputy talk about a training class he had recently attended on "concealed compartment" cars. He talked about some of the profiles and techniques of drug traffickers and how to detect hidden compartments used to conceal contraband within a vehicle. Like most cops who enjoy the chase of the bad guy, I found the aura and mystique of hidden compartment vehicles and the apprehension of a cross country drug trafficker tantalizing.

Most patrol officers would attend a class, be shown pictures of busted hidden compartments in conveyances resulting in ridiculously large seizures of drugs and/or money, ad nausea, then return to their respective departments and begin the quest for a tremendous seizure of their own . . . for about a week.

These seizures are not an everyday occurrence. To find one takes directed attention, on specific routes for long periods of time. The return on investment in anti-drug work can be a lengthy cycle and requires persistence and patience. Patrol officers easily burn out and return focus to normal street-level activity; the easy road.

Fortunately for me, I had a more positive result. The same afternoon shift I heard my co-worker's dissertation, I decided to put myself in a position to intercept one of those interstate traffickers and later that evening, I did. It was more so by dumb luck, than a comprehensive application of any real trained tactics, probably. Nonetheless, I stopped a pick-up truck, that had just arrived in town and, upon noticing a few blatant discrepancies, discovered a hidden compartment in the gas tank of the vehicle. I owe thanks to my now-retired canine partner, Mato, for this apprehension, as I would not have looked in the right place without him pointing me there.

About one week later, Mato and I stopped a motor home, with almost 900 lbs of marijuana in a hidden compartment. Of course, for a cop who loved dope work, I was immediately hooked on these tactics. I began doing research on some previous seizures my canine team had assisted on.

Mato and I conducted what is known as a "probable cause sniff" on hundreds of pounds of marijuana and cocaine for other drug units, that already reasonably knew, based on their investigation, that dope was inside of a vehicle, but needed the legally dependable indication of a narcotic detection dog to conduct the search for the subsequent seizure.

The traffickers I encountered during normal patrol and the ones encountered in response to drug agency requests, all possessed similar interconnecting traits and profiles (important to note: none of which were race).

Soon after these seizures, I began pushing my agency to consider a full-time trafficking detection team. With our jurisdiction positioned just west of Chicago, home to the second largest city in the state, and having two main interstates flowing through it, there were plenty of opportunities to encounter large drug and drug money shipments.

Unfortunately, the idea of focusing police efforts directly on the primary means of illicit drug transportation to the northern regions of the United States is non-traditional. Instead, I was assigned to a street level narcotics unit, and soon I was back to investigating the common crack house and hapless teenager selling dope after school. As I returned to the undercover investigator line of work, I began to see the futility of this brand of drug enforcement.

Crack dealers, street gang members, and 17 year-olds selling weed are a dime-a-dozen. It seemed as if I was spinning my wheels, and making very little headway in stifling these issues on a case by case basis. I rationalized that the interception of the bulk shipment of drugs, as they arrived in the community would immediately handicap all of the aforementioned community concerns in one fell swoop.

The detection of bulk drug trafficking into our neighborhoods is entirely possible, applicable, and trainable. It seems clear that by placing at least one trained and experienced policeman at the gateway to any community, with the task of halting drug influx by observing and detecting trafficking profiles, would be a pragmatic approach. However, the concept of overt drug interdiction on a full-time basis continues to experience roadblocks. "Manpower shortages," "calls for service," "no budget for additional positions" are all reasons that seem to repeatedly trump a dominating response to one of our most vital missions as local police.

As a citizen, I am further concerned with law enforcement's failure to recognize the potential of bulk drug interdiction, and acknowledge the possibility that their tactics are dangerously outdated. To know that other towns, counties, and states across the country are intercepting tremendous loads of narcotics, that would have ultimately ended up on their streets-negatively affecting their crime rate is frustrating to compare to a community that refuses to adopt the same tactic.

As other communities benefit from seizing millions of dollars of drug money headed back to the suppliers, others face detrimental service cuts and civil service lay-offs. Meanwhile, those other towns are lawfully appropriating that money to supplement their services to their citizens. All of our home towns are sitting on a tax-liberating gold mine, whether we capitalize on the opportunity or not, is entirely our choice.

As I began my research for this publication, I started networking with interdiction officers across the country in an attempt to gather numbers to make a stronger case for the dire need for this sort of program in my own community. While speaking with cops from various regions, I became amazed at their success stories of seizing hundreds of pounds of illegal substances in a single stop, and grabbing hundreds of thousands, even millions of dollars of dope cash in just one encounter with a trafficker. Even more engaging were the opportunities that the forfeited drug money allotted the community that the seizing agency served.

I was also astounded to hear the lack of support from some of those officer's agencies, co-workers, and communities. Some interdictors experienced flat-out prohibition from conducting certain activities that were proven crime stoppers and revenue generators for their jurisdiction.

My distress was compounded by the daily reports of cities, counties and states battling multi-million dollar budget deficits, facing layoffs of hundreds of employees and cuts to vital community services. All the while politicians scratched their heads about how to stretch their citizen's tax dollars further or consider a method of increasing taxes to the working class.

Taxes are undeniably important to government function on all levels, BUT they are not a government's sole source of income. Viable alternatives exist to make their ends meet. Especially when they have a police agency poised to create substantial monetary gain for itself, resulting in substantial gain for the community.

I rationalized that one reason why any law enforcement agency, any police officer, or any community would dispute massive seizures of the substance that supports America's criminal culture may be a lack of information. A compilation of facts and statistics must be made available to the public for everyone to have a clear understanding of the effects of drugs on our country. The numbers presented must have supporting evidence from agencies that dedicate their personnel to the cause of contraband interception at the corridor to the community, and presently experience substantial dividends from those practices.

I set out to create this compilation as a call to arms for all readers: the police officer, the house wife, and the businessman. As people and governments set down their arms, in surrender to the current stronghold of the drug culture, the facts and details of my writing seek to underline the vital importance of a specific brand of drug enforcement that is truly the missing link in the American police forces' battle against crime.

It is the core function of your local government and police agency to serve and protect you. They must be responsive to your needs and requests. Every resident of every community has a voice with their governing body. If your police agency is not operating with these priorities in mind, it is your obligation to ask them why they are not employing all of the resources at their disposal to eradicate drugs and crime, and relieve tax dollars, by supporting themselves with seized illicit funds.

As proof in action, I sought out the three men who originated these tactics and techniques decades ago, and whose lives were and are dedicated to this unique brand of police work. These men are the pioneers for what is destined to be America's answer to the "War on Drugs". Their inception into this cause, and the results of their labor, are the foundation of the limitless possibilities of this important mission.

The sum of this unique policing strategy will demonstrate the untapped efficiency in the protection of our land and borders from all brands of criminal activity. The ethical application of these proactive tactics, through a structured training regimen may virtually eliminate the perceived need to create constitutionally invasive immigration laws that have sparked many recent protests.

The powerful results of police officers emboldened with these skills will demonstrate the ability of local law enforcement to lead the fight against terrorism on our own soil, eliminating the need for multi-billion dollar wars abroad.

We can save a multitude of lives, create and retain American jobs, and cut crimes that affect us all, directly or indirectly, on a daily basis. It also facilitates the all-important detection of international and domestic terrorism in the United States.

Ultimately, we as a nation, owe our dedication to this cause for the sake of Michael York, Robert Rehm, and many other American youth who die senselessly every day due to our cumulative failure to properly address the "war on drugs." We must stop the cliché that this effort has become. We must be willing to adapt and overcome. The enemy is identifiable, the weapons are available, the troops are standing by; the time is now.

JUST THE FACTS . . .

"These are the times that try men's souls. The summer soldier and the sunshine patriot will, in this crisis, shrink from the service of their country; but he that stands it now, deserves the love and thanks of man and woman. Tyranny, like hell, is not easily conquered; yet we have this consolation with us, that the harder the conflict, the more glorious the triumph. What we obtain too cheap, we esteem too lightly; it is dearness only that gives everything its value. I love the man that can smile in trouble, that can gather strength from distress and grow brave by reflection."

-Thomas Paine

During the economic strife of 2009 and 2010, the national unemployment rate hovered around 10%[ii]. We clenched onto our wallets and our personal possessions, waiting to see if the paycheck would come at the end of the week. Our country's financial system seemed on the brink of disaster and the old saying, "it's gonna get worse before its gets better" served as the running subtitle for every economist's television editorial.

Meanwhile, there was another region of American commerce that had never suffered a down-turn, since its surge in the 1960's: the international drug trade. The movement of cocaine, heroin, marijuana, and methamphetamine from the warm tropical climates of the south to urban and suburban America has thrived under all economic conditions. This industry even takes an upturn in down economies, as out-of-work citizens turn to desperate measures to make ends meet.

The margins in this business model are a dream come true for any corporate American, stock market trader, or entrepreneur. The demand for the product has always remained high. The supply has constantly flowed and the logistics have adapted and improved, always overcoming any temporary setbacks.

During a stable economy, a steady flow of illegal immigrants and unemployable ex-con's are available to participate in the movement and distribution chains of illicit drugs. In a down market, unemployed workers are often tempted by the quick dollar and offer themselves to the trafficking network as well. The reward for them can be handsome, in the form of thousands of untaxed dollars per transaction. Their risk lies in associating themselves with the black market and the inherent dangers of dealing with drug cartel affiliates. Ironically, the risk of facing police interdiction is minimal.

It is estimated that US law enforcement seizes less than 1% of all illicit narcotics that flow into our country[iii]. Imagine a legitimate corporation that has an over 99% success rate on sales from their delivered goods. They would have some rather content investors. Such is the life of the drug cartels.

While this industry booms and police (by and large) scratch their heads at the influx, many argue, "It's just dope . . . don't we have far more serious things to worry about like murder, rape, robbery?" Considering the cause and effect relationship that illicit narcotics have on murder, rape and robbery, I deem this logic moot.

In a 2008 Arrestee Drug Abuse Monitoring (ADAM) Study of detainees held at adult detention centers in major U.S. cities; 87% of adult inmates tested positive for a narcotic after being booked for a crime. This statistic, alone, speaks volumes on the impact of illegal drugs on our society. Almost 90% of those who commit the crimes that make us shudder at the nightly news or gasp in disbelief as they occur in our neighborhoods, are apparently created by (or at least strongly linked to) a single, identifiable cause: illicit drugs. This scientific finding of the ADAM study is arguably the most significant calculation in the measurement of illicit drugs' impact on our society.[xxiii]

Consider the biggest monsters of them all: serial killers. A link between drug abuse and their behavior is apparent throughout their violent lives. Just a few for example: John Wayne Gacy, who raped and murdered thirty-three young men between 1972 and 1978; Jeffery Dahmer, murdered seventeen men and boys in his reign of terror; and Brian Dugan, from the Chicago area, who raped and murdered two girls and one adult woman, all used and abused narcotics.

Their drug use was highlighted in court testimony in each of their trials as being a source of their psychological disconnect or as a un-inhibitor, allowing them to commit their crimes without hesitation or clarity.

One of the most notorious killers in American history, Charles Manson, utilized controlled substances, in order to entrance his minions and provoke them into killing on his behalf. Manson followers would also indulge on a non-inhibitor, usually cocaine during the commission of the murders, to ensure they would follow through with their leader's commands.

Yet, many of the psychologists who examine their behavior, brain patterns, and speech cues, never rest on one common thread: habitual, hard-core drug use. It begs the question; what if there was more emphasis on drug enforcement or general proactive criminal patrol by police in the areas where those vile crimes were committed? What if more contact was made with these killers by law enforcement in the course of their normal drug enforcement duties?

Could police have deterred these men from their crimes? Could patrolmen have cut off their supply chain, seizing claim to their substances of empowerment, thereby stopping their will to act (as well as their freedom) if incarcerated?

Of course, the answer to these hypotheses we will never know. It is possible to reason, however that if you attack and deter the primary link to violent criminal offenders, you stand a good chance of attacking and deterring their detrimental effects on the lives of innocent people.

Outside of high-profile violent crimes committed under the influence of narcotics, chances are that the majority of Americans have felt the effects of drugs in their community. If you've ever been a victim of a car or home burglary, a mugging, robbery, or a financial identity theft, you can reasonably assume that the person committing those offenses and the money being sought through the commission of those crimes are connected, in some fashion, to the drug trade (87% of the time).

Drug crimes, as defined by the Office of Bureau of Justice Statistics, are thrown into three categories:

d*rug-defined offenses*: "the violations of laws prohibiting or regulating the possession, distribution, or manufacture of illegal drugs."

d*rug-related offenses:* "offenses in which drug's pharmacologic effects contribute; offenses are motivated by the user's need for money to support continued use; and offenses connected to drug distribution itself."

drug-using lifestyle: "drug use and crime are common aspects of a deviant lifestyle. The likelihood and frequency of involvement in illegal activity is increased because drug users may not participate in the legitimate economy and are exposed to situations that encourage crime."

Definitions may be dry reading, but try this game with your morning newspaper. Open it to the police blotter section and review the criminal activity in your community. Chances are you can plug each incident into at least one heading listed above.

Let us not forget another analysis of America's core violence concern: the common street gang. We, as a nation, have complained about these militant groups since the 1950's. The Chicagoland "Vice Lords" enjoy the title of America's first street gang, and were established under extortionist principles. They quickly discovered the benefits of drug trade and thus boomed the street gang/drug dealing culture.

From the Mexican Mafia of California, to the Latin Kings of the Midwest and East coast, the Bloods and Crips of Los Angeles to the Gangster Disciples of

Chicago, illicit drug sales are, and have been, the bread and butter of street gangs.

As gangs battle for drug territory, and innocent by-standers are gunned down, we are left shaking our heads at the 10 o'clock news. But, again, what is the root of all this unnecessary violence? Illicit drugs (87% of the time)!

The publication, "Freakonomics," authored by Steven D. Levitt and Stephen J. Dubner, described the financial structure of the Chicago "Gangster Disciple" drug-trade as an organized and corporate endeavor. The publication leant much to the fascination and productivity of the gangsters' cause, but little to the massive violence and lawlessness that surrounded their activities.

The story featured in "Freakonomics" is an excellent example of the American dismissal of this prevalent sub-culture. The illegal drug trade and use in our communities has become such a cliché that it is almost accepted as the norm. Meanwhile, United States citizens are violated by crimes driven by illegal narcotics each day. Criminal justice and elected officials struggle to pin-point causes, and spend billions of dollars in responsive investigations, trying to play political hot potato with their community's safety concerns.

The statistic that 87% of all incarcerated people are under the influence of a narcotic at the time of their arrest is a clear common denominator for the cause of American crime. So what is the cumulative response to this primary identifiable source by the American police force?

The "War" on Drugs

"In the truest sense, freedom cannot be bestowed; it must be achieved."

-Franklin D. Roosevelt

The dictionary definition of *war* is described as an active struggle between competing entities. We could argue that the drug cartels, pouring hundreds of pounds of cannabis and metric tons of cocaine (as described by the ONDCP Clearinghouse) and heroin onto our streets are competing entities with our police forces. Considering the single fact that American police seize only 1% of those drugs being trafficked into our communities, the "competition" for the trafficking organizations is minimal.

Webster's Dictionary defines *invasion* as an intrusion that directly threatens the autonomy of a nation or territory. The importation, trafficking, and use of illicit drugs in America remains a severe attack on our "autonomy."

The Center for Disease Control estimated that illicit drug use costs our nation $161 billion per year in lost revenue. Billions of dollars flow from our economy to foreign drug markets, with no return. Our national revenue is bilked by lost work productivity, extensive treatment programs for both medical and psychological conditions, incarceration, and criminal processing costs.

Knowing these initial basic statistics, we can purport that the "war" is-being lost, but it is not over . . . and there is a way to turn the tide. Who should lead this revolution?

Federal agencies, such as the FBI and DEA, are seen as our front lines in this invasion. However, the numbers are not stacked in their favor. Consider the US Border Patrol. The numbers fluctuate on a daily basis, but generally speaking; greater than 500,000 people cross the US/Mexico border every day. Crossing agents have approximately 7 seconds to decide whether or not to send an incoming vehicle into a "search" lane or allow them to pass on to the streets of America[iv].

If the vehicle is deferred to the search lane, then the agents must work to discover which one of the millions of different clever methods the courier has used to conceal his contraband. All the while, due to the mass of traffic, many other vehicles are allowed to pass through, loaded with narcotics, destined for our neighborhoods.

This daunting task for border agents only considers inbound drug shipments crossing through a legitimate border checkpoint. There are a total 1,969 miles of border between the United States and Mexico. Daily runs for the border are made through the desert or water (the Rio Grande) with loads of illegal immigrants or the real money maker: drugs.

U.S. Border Patrol agents do a fantastic job with the resources provided, for the vast area they need to cover, but based on immigration and narcotic numbers alone, they cannot possibly curb it all.

Local field agents for DEA are typically tasked with long duration, in-depth investigations into trafficking groups or individuals. These investigations require hundreds of personnel hours for multiple agents to draw lengthy reports and court documents, and while they may uncover one-time large shipments of illicit drugs, the detail of their work is so involved that they are only able to tackle a tiny fraction of the market before their case is concluded. Federal agents must then start from scratch on the next smuggling group, while another molds into place where the last was dismantled.

The United States' government's international priority also appears to lie in the Global War on Terror, and not the narco-terrorism that impacts us on a daily basis. Since the initiation of the conflicts in Iraq and Afghanistan, America has spent $10.9 billion per month on our military deployments[v].

Meanwhile, in 2009, US Congress approved the Merida Initiative which provides $1.4 billion to Central American countries for drug enforcement operations[vi]. That is $1.4 billion . . . over the course of three years.

By way of comparison on national impact; 2,973 Americans died during the September 11th attacks that initiated our global war on terror; annual US government responsive expenditure: $130.8 billion.

An average of 15,000 Americans die from illicit drug-induced deaths[vii] EACH YEAR; annual US government responsive expenditure: $466 million.

While it is of high importance to seek Al Qaeda members and other terrorist cells to protect our nation's interest, at home and abroad; it is important to note that the federal government is most-likely not positioned to be the sole (or even the primary) combatant in the "War on Drugs."

Based on personnel numbers alone, the assets needed to begin a much more pragmatic initiative to the American drug war are already in place. Our thin blue lines in the war against our nation's principle crime producer are the uniformed patrol officers, deputies, and state troopers driving the highways and bi-ways of our home towns every day.

So why have they yet to make an impact? Where are these assets directed now and how can they be re-directed for the betterment of a nation?

POLICE NUMBERS

"This nation will remain the land of the free only so long as it is the home if the brave."

-Elmer Davis

Knowing those basic facts and numbers previously discussed we can identify a high priority, if not the single most important priority, in modern American policing: the drug "war."

A centuries-old source for assessing approaches and tactics in any conflict is found in the writings of the ancient Chinese warrior, Sun Tzu. Sun Tzu writes, "If ignorant both of your enemy and yourself, you are certain to be in peril". In the same work, he writes, "Know thy self, know thy enemy. A thousand battles, a thousand victories."[viii]

Know the problem, know your resources available in solving the problem, then successfully solve it.

Yet on average, only 5% of the personnel in local, county, and state police agencies are specifically tasked with narcotic enforcement. In Illinois alone, there are 38,179 police officers; only an estimated 1,900 officers are trained and directed on drug detection[ix]. Only five percent of Illinois police officers are directed to stop the crimes that create almost 90% of the evil in our society.

Compare Microsoft's 55,000 United States employees to our country's largest police force: the New York Police Department, with approximately 36,000 sworn personnel. The Microsoft Corporation's annual report for 2008 showed that their Microsoft Office Systems result in 90% of the revenue for their Business Division.

Imagine if Microsoft only dedicated about 5% of its work force to the Microsoft Office Systems. This would contradict all common-sense business practices. If you have an area of obvious dominance that can be further developed through persistent attention, you assign as many of your high-performance employees to the division. You also encourage employees providing support to that division to prioritize their resources accordingly to ensure continued success.

If Microsoft only chose to dedicate 5% or less of their staff to the region of the business that claimed 90% of the revenue, what would be the outcome? We could assume the worst in customer service, product deterioration, and resource overload.

As a military comparison, President Barack Obama decided in December of 2009 to send 30,000 additional troops to support the American war efforts in Afghanistan. Of those 30,000 soldiers; approximately 5,000 were trainers and support staff. About 25,000 of them were infantry personnel; the men designed and trained to bring an immediate and definitive end to resistance.

Knowing that the war in Afghanistan involved a great deal of technical searching and warfare to weed out the Taliban and Al-Qaeda gorillas seeded deep in the Hindu-Kush mountains, you might imagine the impact of sending 30,000 troops, but with the assignments swapped.

The U.S. would be plugging in only 5,000 additional men to navigate and battle through the rugged terrain, while 25,000 troops supported them from behind the scenes or conducted other nonaggressive military duties pertaining to the US/Afghan occupation.

This would contradict the inherent tactic to place the concentrated effort on the primary concern. It would also cause an almost certain loss of the war efforts. This, essentially, is what we face in the police "war" on drugs. How can we, as a nation, expect to win a "war" when we fail to engage all of our "soldiers" in its cause?

Still, some may argue there are federal agencies in place, specifically the Drug Enforcement Administration (DEA), to handle the threat of narco-terrorism. For the major city of a State that the DEA website claims: "is the major transportation hub and distribution center for illegal drugs throughout the Midwest, due to its geographic location and multi-faceted transportation infrastructure," consider this 2006 Illinois statistic: DEA field offices accounted for 996 drug arrests, while local law enforcement accounted for 112,368 drug seizures the same year.

Which agent of the law has demonstrated the higher propensity to come in contact with the criminals tunneling drugs through our streets? Your local police officer.

The Drug Enforcement Administration routinely executes elaborate stings and drag nets that have international ramifications on the illegal drug trade. But the American street patrol officer is the final line of defense and is statistically proven to have the highest frequency of contact with narcotic traffickers.

The Office of National Drug Control Policy states on their website that, "Drug trafficking organizations based in Mexico transport metric-ton quantities of cocaine from the southwest border into Illinois, primarily to Chicago, on a regular basis."

But again, only 5% of the local police in that state are specifically directed to combat illicit narcotics. Should this not be priority number "1" of all of Illinois' police forces? Should the training on drug trends and trafficking profiles not be annually mandated much like training on first aid and CPR for our first responders?

The crimes created by illicit narcotics dominate the concerns of our citizens, but the drugs, themselves, continue not to be the priority of many of our police forces. This singularly dominating precursor of illegal activity needs to be the primary focus of all local law enforcement as evidenced by their 99% margin over federal agents in encountering drugs.

During a study of drug crime on the community I served, I conducted a survey of one hundred local police officers. I knew from my experience that most uniformed patrol officers did not particularly prioritize the aggressive pursuit of drug law violators during their daily functions. However, I wanted to know what their perceptions were regarding the effects that illicit narcotics had on their towns and counties.

The following is the survey questions, with their multiple choice answers. The answer receiving the highest mark is highlighted and underlined, with the percentage of those who chose that answer:

Question #1

How often do you receive training in narcotics and narcotic enforcement?

Once every . . .

*Monthly or less months

*2-6 months

* 6 - 1 2

*12-18 months

18 months or more (60%)

Question #2

How often do you receive information on current narcotic trafficking trends specific to your town or county?

Once every . . .

*Monthly or less months

*2-6 months

* 6 - 1 2

*12-18 months

18 months or more (41%)

Question #3

How do you view your roll in illicit drug enforcement?

*Relentlessly pursue narcotic arrests

*Occasionally pursue narcotic arrests (41%)

*Some interest in narcotic arrests

*Little or no interest in narcotic arrests

Question #4

How do you perceive your agency's/supervisor's disposition toward patrol officers making drug arrests?

*Strongly encourage arrests

*Allow arrests, but no specific encouragement (46%)

*Encourage other efforts more than drug detection

*Discourage drug detection

Question #5

Based on your experience and belief, narcotics account for what percentage of crime (this includes crime committed while the offenders are under the influence or crimes which may be linked to the purchase or sale of drugs)?

*Less than 20%

*21-40%

*41-60% (40%)

*61-80%

*81-100%

Officers from twelve separate jurisdictions in the Chicagoland area were polled in this study. Understandably, this survey cannot speak for local law enforcement across the country, but the results can lend insight to the lack of emphasis on drug detection efforts by the men and women who are best poised to perform the task.

The majority of officers stated they do not receive narcotics-related training or training specific to drug trends in the communities they serve on a routine basis. An officer, who by the nature of their employment is civilly and criminally culpable for their actions in so many regards-cannot effectively operate in an enforcement theater without specific, reliable, and consistent training on any given topic. Especially the topic that creates 87% of the issues they face every day.

Law enforcement administrators are accountable to the people who pay their salaries-the American citizen. The primary function of local police should be the unwavering focus on the issue creating the bulk of the crime that affects John Q. Public's daily life.

The National Association of Drug Enforcement Officers mission statement is as follows: "to promote the cooperation, education, and exchange of information among all Law Enforcement Agencies involved in the enforcement of controlled substance laws."

More narrowly, the State of Illinois maintains the Illinois Drug Enforcement Officers Association whose motto states, "The membership is composed of those sworn law enforcement officers whose primary responsibility is the enforcement of narcotics laws in the State of Illinois".

The focus of their membership is on the minuscule percentage of officers assigned to full-time drug detection groups. With the present-day impact of drugs on crime, isn't it the responsibility of all policemen to be included and trained in fighting this battle?

These national and state organizations are in position to lead the charge in identifying the problem, training the solutions, and engaging everyone to focus their resources in the right direction. Unfortunately, their training seminars more closely resemble a fraternity party and their teachings are relatively archaic in approach and technique.

Fortunately for American law enforcement, revolutionary alternatives exist that present a real, tangible, and proven approach to executing large scale blows to the international drug trade. Enter the web-based training and networking center for local law enforcement: "Desert Snow."

Desert Snow/Black Asphalt features a blog section that displays up-to-the-minute information for all police officers on drug-trafficking profiles, trends, and identifiers. An officer can even learn the amount and type of illicit drugs traveling to or from one specific location to another.

Out of the over 683,000 local law enforcement officers in the United States, just over 30,000 officers belong to this web site. Only 3% of American Police Officers monitor this free, convenient and undeniably crucial internet portal.

The specific information contained within this site is designed for one specific facet of drug enforcement: the interdiction of bulk drug loads and currency bundles as they travel from source to source. Let me repeat . . . only 3% of American law enforcement monitors this activity!

The majority of personnel assigned to "drug enforcement groups" are concentrating on the crack houses, street dealers, and teenage weed retailers. It seems painfully obvious that if only a small percentage of personnel can be dedicated, why not concentrate them on cutting off the head of the proverbial cobra? The focus must be placed on the main, identifiable means by which drugs arrive on our streets, and in your children's schools on a daily basis. Summarily, once the main artery (the in-road) is severed, the entire system bleeds out.

DOLLARS

"Valor delights in the test"

Roman Proverb

While some may hold out on acknowledging the negative effects of illicit drugs on our communities or the dire importance of police emphasis on narcotic crimes, most can appreciate the staggering money transfer involved in the international drug trade, especially during a struggling economy. The 2009 National Drug Threat Assessment calculated that $18 to $39 billion of United States Currency is out of circulation in foreign drug markets.

With metric-ton quantities of cocaine, marijuana and heroin spilling onto the streets of America, the money that drives the supply has to be collected and returned to those who provide the product.

Aurora, Illinois, the second largest city in the state, with a population of over 170,000 people, shares the dubious distinction by federal and local law enforcement as being recognized as an international drug hub with its neighbor, Chicago.

Based on local one-time drug seizures and the estimates of federal and local police working the area, conservative calculations indicate that

37

approximately 500 lbs to 1,000 lbs of marijuana are smuggled into the town, per week. Also, between thirty and forty kilograms of cocaine are trafficked in during the same period[x].

Considering the typical bulk price per pound of cannabis is hovering around $500; and a large shipment of cocaine would cost approximately $27,000 per kilogram; then this second city returns between $1,060,000 and $1,580,000 to the foreign drug markets every week.

Over $1,000,000 per week returned to foreign drug markets from just one, relatively small, town.

Chicago holds an estimated 20% share in the U.S. illicit drug trade[xi]. Therefore, Chicago would lose about $3.6 billion (20% of $18 billion), annually, in out-flowing drug money. Very conservatively estimating that Aurora would own about 20% of the Chicago area stock, Aurora's annual loss would equal $720,000,000 or $13,846,153 per week. Even more staggering than the calculated estimate based on drug flow!

Bulk US currency discovered in a stash house

While many municipal, county, and state governments face devastating budget cuts and layoffs of crucial personnel, these massive amounts of money continue to flow out of their jurisdictions. Based on state and federal laws, the laundering and concealed transport of this currency allows forfeit of the cash and subsequent award to the seizing law enforcement agency for use in budget augmentation. The same techniques used by those very few drug trafficking interceptors for detecting bulk drug distribution can be used to interdict the laundering of drug cash.

For those local police agencies that have taken notice and dedicated their personnel to interception activities, the rewards have been tremendous. For example, during the first month of 2010, some of these uniquely trained patrolmen and women from varying agencies in the United States made contact with people arriving in or passing through their communities.

In these one-on-one encounters, patrolmen seized massive amounts of currency as a result of their attention to duty and detail. In just one week during that January, Desert Snow-trained interceptors made money seizures that will feed their agencies and, by benefactor, their citizens for a substantial period of time.

On the 21st, a Sheriff's Deputy in Kansas took $1,017,183 from a vehicle. A few days later on the 25th, a Kansas deputy from a separate agency nabbed $590,000 cash, during another traffic stop. On the eastern half of the country on the 26th, a Georgia deputy laid siege on $543,797 in currency.[xxiv] Shortly thereafter, Georgia's close neighbor, North Carolina, is the proud home to a local patrolman whose watchful eye led to the capture of $1,104,280 on the

28th. The same car also happened to be transporting 1,082 lbs of marijuana.

Through mandates of states and federal drug asset forfeiture and money laundering statutes, police forces are one of the only government entities that can generate revenue for the community they serve. However, traffic tickets-in-mass are not the answer. Trained drug trafficking interception and ethical narcotic currency forfeiture is the proven foundation for a self-supporting local agency.

Generally speaking, seizing police entities receive 80% of the total forfeited cash. Imagine the North Carolinian village as an example. Once awarded their share of the $1 million-plus seizure, they will receive roughly $883,000. This money can only be used by the police agency and (depending on the statute the money was seized under) only for drug enforcement-related operations and equipment.

If this law enforcement agency aligned their assets at the primary cause of the crime they respond to (drugs), they could justify using the seized drug money to support a myriad of services they provide. In turn, imagine if the police department appropriated $800,000 of their tax-supplied budget back to their city's general fund following judicial appropriation of the seizure money. This one North Carolina encounter could serve to finance numerous other city functions, services, and pay checks by association.

The drug trade has proven to be recession proof. Americans have the assets to capitalize on this industry and handsomely support public services during times of strife. The opportunity is there, the resources are in place, the training is available.

THE FRONTIER

*"We sleep safe in our beds because rough men stand
ready in the night to visit violence on those who would bring
us harm."*

-George Orwell

Since the days of Miami Vice, America has been
exposed to the glamorous world of undercover cops
chasing down bad guys and dope dealers. Many
local police agencies sprouted task forces that were
the inspiration for such television shows, to battle
the formidable opponents of cocaine, heroin, crack
cocaine and the methamphetamine family.

By the early 1970's, street narcotics already had
an overwhelming grip on our urban areas. At the
inception of these street-level counter drug units,
the tail-chasing was immediate. While one "network"
of traffickers was dismantled by police, three other
groups were operating within a half-mile of that
network. As officers moved on to tackle the next,
nearby group, another nefarious entrepreneur would
step up with his associates and take the place of the
recently removed group.

Working at the street nickel-and-dime dealer level
presents an endless chore for law enforcement.
Thousands and thousands of personnel hours (tax

dollars) a year are spent on these officers to work in this arena of crime. As the evidence shows, police are badly losing the war on drugs. Essentially, they are barely putting up a fight.

Beginning in the mid-1980's, American law enforcement gave birth to a new solution to the epidemic. A small group of crime-fighters working in unassuming assignments in jurisdictions far from the asphalt jungles began making serious dents in the flow of drugs across America. Mostly through happen-stance encounters, these officers started piecing together the puzzle of drug trafficking techniques and profiles.

For some, it was an encounter with a suspicious motorist while on routine patrol, during which the officer detected something was afoot and pushed the investigation further.

For others, the drugs almost literally landed in their lap, causing a "eureka" moment that altered the course of their career. In either scenario, these few men had two things in common: a heightened sense of awareness to the influx of illicit drugs and an intense drive to better themselves and the community they served by attacking the flow as it traversed America's arteries.

At the point of inception to this cause, these patrollers were unaware how firmly they would shape what is now the tip of the spear in our country's battle against dangerous drugs. These forefathers of bulk drug interception crafted, designed, and perfected their art. They demonstrated plausible, ethical methods of drug network destabilization and contraband concealment detection.

After striking out against our national epidemic with the trafficking profiles they defined and the techniques they mastered, these pioneers would transfer this power of knowledge to thousands of patrolmen scattered across the country.

Telling the tales of their early successes and capturing the passionate drive these men, their families, and their disciples continue to feel for this cause is imperative in portraying the necessity of and urgency in implementing these policing techniques. As the biographies reveal, the undeniable evidence of the fruits of their labor is the driving force behind one of the most important American anti-crime initiatives.

JOE DAVID

*"It is better to live one day as a lion
than one hundred years as a sheep."*

-Roman Adage

The uniformed policing world in the early 1980's was depicted and immortalized by drama series like "T.J. Hooker", "21 Jump Street" and "CHiP's." So what better location to start than southern California? As for the influx of drugs into North America, southern California also makes for an appropriate point of origin.

Enter Joe David. Hired by the California Highway Patrol in 1985, Joe assumed the traditional roles of a Highway Patrolmen. He worked the inconspicuous rural roads of the far south-eastern portion of the state responding to emergency calls, writing traffic tickets, and assisting disabled motorists. Joe recalled that ideas of drug enforcement or drug detection, in general, for a highway patrolman were non-existent. But Joe maintained the inquisitive nature of any good police officer when engaged in his duties.

The propensity to question everything and dig deeper at the first sign of suspicion is the cornerstone of a true career law dog. And so begins a life's passion on a stretch of highway in Needles, CA, circa 1986. As I mentioned, many of these pioneers began their incredible campaign against international drug traffickers by a chance encounter, and Joe is no different in that regard.

One sultry desert afternoon, Joe came upon a broken down Ford Thunderbird on the side of the highway while on routine patrol. The Trooper struck up a conversation with the two fellows in the car and quickly became aware that something was not quite right. Another Highway Patrolman came along to check on Joe while he was conversing with the men.

Thinking the motorists may be attempting to conceal some fruit of a crime from him, he asked the men for permission to search the T-bird. The men quickly and confidently gave Joe the go-ahead. Trooper

David dove into the car, determined to peel back the layers of this proverbial onion and figure out what these guys were up to.

Admittedly, Joe did not really know what he was looking for, but he simply knew something was not right. After intently searching the insides of the vehicle, but finding nothing, Joe's frustrations grew. As he sweated over the details of the T-Bird, he noticed a passerby had stopped and was out of his car, talking to Joe's partner. This being an occasional annoyance (even a hazard) for patrolmen, Joe took a break to check in with the other Trooper.

Oddly enough, the motorist had stopped because he recognized the assisting Trooper as a classmate from high school twenty years earlier. Joe put his road-side venture on pause for a moment and joined in the conversation between his partner and the passing motorist. He asked the old classmate what he was doing for a living. The man explained that he was working as an upholsterer, mostly for cars and trucks.

Finding a moment of fate, a smile spread on Joe's face and he invited the man to come join in on his pursuit. Joe's new assistant examined the car, and noticed a few imperfections and oddities about the composition of the vehicle's interior. After a couple pulls and pushes, twenty kilograms of cocaine were removed from inside the broken-down T-bird.

One of the two motorists, turned suspects, Joe found in the car, happened to hold the influential rank of Lieutenant for the Medellín Cartel.[xxv] The Medellín, founded by the infamous Pablo Escobar, was a notorious organization who operated in the 1970's and 80's in Columbia, Bolivia, Peru, Central

America, United States, Canada, and Europe. It is estimated the Medellín trafficked about $60 million per day in narcotics, mainly cocaine.

Joe jokes that immediately following the stop, he phoned the local Drug Enforcement Administration office and informed them that the "war" (meaning America's War on Drugs) was over. Fortunately, he realized this was only the beginning and from that day forward, the Medellín would be the primary target of Joe David's intense drive for drug interception.

Having nabbed 44 pounds of cocaine out of the T-bird after a chance encounter with an upholsterer, Joe was immediately addicted to the cat-and-mouse game of trafficker detection.

Trooper David became a one-man wrecking ball, and terrorized members of drug cartels for years to come. He even set up a mapping system of Medellín movements through southern California on the walls of his bedroom. In 1988, Joe made a record seizure of 2,500 lbs of cocaine rolling down the highway in the back of a box truck. To put this in financial perspective, that amount of cocaine had a street value of over $22 million dollars.

Joe David's 2,500 kilo find

Narcotic units, assigned solely to investigating drug crimes, can work for decades with multiple detectives and never encounter this much contraband. For instance, an organized drug unit consisting of 16 investigators working in Cook County, IL (the home of Chicago) worked for an entire year in 2009 and came up with 138 kilograms (303 lbs) of cocaine. For statistical averaging, in 2008 the same group working in this international drug hub which receives "metric ton quantities of cocaine" seized 113 kilograms (248 lbs) of the same drug[xii].

Mind you, these statistics are considered above average for a local drug investigation group. But in single officer encounters, multiple times over the course of a year, Joe was blowing numbers like these out of the water.

These strategies, although cutting-edge at the time, continue to be refuted and ignored as a hit-or-miss tactic by many law enforcement administrators across the nation to this day. Meanwhile, in scattered domains across the nation, Joe's disciples relentlessly throw up similar seizure numbers during one-on-one encounters utilizing his principles.

The tactic of drug influx interception utilizes readily available resources (local police) armed with the training and experience to clot the hemorrhage of narcotics at the point of insertion to our communities. Joe was destined to be the purveyor of this golden information, starting in southwestern America.

In the mid-1980's, Joe was developing and fine-tuning policing strategies that were making indelible marks in the war on drugs and, while this pioneer was striking out on the front lines during the day, by night he began holding court during backyard barbeques. Police officers from jurisdictions around southern California started coming to Joe's house to listen to the war stories in hopes of picking up some tactics to deploy on their own.

Fairly quickly, these beer-drinking casual gatherings rolled from the barbeque pit to a little more formal and hospitable venue in Joe's garage. More and more law enforcement officers attended these congregations, on their own time, in an attempt to arm themselves with the powerful weapon of knowledge and experience.

Just like Joe, these men from agencies across California and Arizona saw the detrimental effects that illicit drugs were having on their communities. They saw that gaining the information necessary to detect and intercept the mules carrying the contraband into our society for the narco-terrorists was the most efficient means in deterring the influx. These patrolmen realized that they were sitting on the front lines of the "war" everyday.

By the nature of their duties, they were and are the sentry at the gates, the overt watchers and keepers of our nation's peace and serenity. They knew that the answer for truly fighting crime did not lie in picking on the high school kids passing the joint around the car and the low-life crack dealers and pipe smokers. Nor was it in preying upon the public behind their speed radar gun.

These pioneers realized there is one vital course of action for the local police officer to begin conquering our nation's continuing battle: knowledge, training in profiles, and the relentless pursuit of narcotic smugglers. With these criterions, Joe David was leading the charge.

In 1993, Joe formalized "Desert Snow." Still primarily based out of his garage, Joe conducted law enforcement classes designed to train police officers from across the nation on the tactics he developed through his own relentless pursuits. Not until Joe was forced into retirement from the Highway Patrol in 2003, due to injury, did his training organization truly take off.

Desert Snow/Black Asphalt now has over 30,000 members (still less than 3% of all uniformed police officers in America), and continues to train local law enforcement on the tactics needed to combat narco-terrorism. What's more, due to the unique and potent content disseminated in these training courses, Desert Snow also receives funding from Homeland Security because it is federally recognized that the tactics and awareness used in fighting narcotic trafficking on the local level, are the same tactics and awareness used in fighting international and domestic terrorism.

As Joe continues to lead the law enforcement community into the new millennium through his vital training, he continues to notice the lack of overall involvement on a national level. From the origin of his cause inside that T-bird on that southern California highway to the back yard cook-outs to the multi-million dollar organization he heads today, Joe has fought for this law enforcement initiative because, as he humbly sees it, "it's just the right thing to do".

Fortunately for America, Joe will continue to pressure police administrations, local governments, military and even congress to make this training and patrol technique more inclusive to all forms of law enforcement in the United States. The communities, whose officers have intercepted large quantities of contraband as it arrived in their town and also enjoyed the benefits of enhanced public services due to financial independence provided by drug money seizures, owe a large "thank you" to Joe David for continuing to do the "right thing".

THE STATUS QUO

"Freedom is never more than one generation away from extinction. We didn't pass it to our children in the bloodstream. It must be fought for, protected, and handed on for them to do the same."

-Ronald Reagan

As highlighted by the last "forefather," the concept and techniques of intercepting the deliveries as they arrive in and pass through any given area of the country are tried and true. They have been in practice (unfortunately, on a very small scale) for decades. These proven techniques used by local law enforcement have also shown to supersede the tail-chasing grind of common police drug units.

Many stories are published in local papers across the nation of police narcotic squads conducting lengthy undercover stings, using thousands of man-hours and resources netting a dozen suspects and a relatively small amount of illegal substances (compared to Joe David's numbers), when several more rings are operating in a similar fashion within the next ten blocks.

A December, 2009, Tempe, Arizona news release shared the story of a Tempe Police Department bust that netted a substantial amount of methamphetamine, cocaine, and heroin; the amount of which was valued at $7 million. The operation resulted in the capture of 130 drug dealers and took months of undercover operations to infiltrate the organization. In all, this mission had a very noteworthy outcome. Contrarily, the police agency admitted during a press conference that this entire effort was most likely just a "drop in the bucket."[xiii]

To weigh the benefits of an investigation of this type, we must consider the amount of government man hours, resources, and benefits (supported by tax dollars) that were spent in such a lengthy, in-depth operation.

To execute arrests on 130 defendants, we could assume that a minimum of over 100 police officers would need to be mobilized to safely and effectively carry out the mission. Considering the median annual police salary of around $61,000[xiv] and that the investigation took nine months to build involving at least twenty detectives; the payroll would cost approximately $915,000. Finally, there was an additional $2,033,300 price tag for the one week apprehension period involving the 100 officer dragnet that was ultimately "just a drop in the bucket."

Seizing dangerous substances in that amount is of definite benefit to the Tempe community. But what if every police officer, not just those assigned to investigative units, was given the training and the direction to root out the couriers of the drugs as they transport them into and through the city?

Consider the following breakdown from the city's investigation: the $7 million in controlled substances were listed as 145 lbs of methamphetamine, 114 lbs of cocaine, and 7 ounces of heroin. Compare that to the period between December 2009 and February 2010 when local and state patrolmen utilizing those specific, trainable interception techniques seized 154 lbs of meth, 759 lbs of cocaine, and 17 lbs of heroin during one-on-one routine traffic stops or consensual encounters[xv].

Which is more economically effective to Tempe: having a multitude of officers working countless hours on a single trafficking organization or having every patrol officer receive precise training on the detection of these traffickers and direct them to interdict the traffickers as they traverse the roads of their city every day?

According to the Tempe Police Department's 2009 Annual Report, there were 561 police personnel working the streets for that fiscal year. The cost per officer for one Desert Snow class is just under $1,000, a $561,000 investment for the training that will repeatedly pay gigantic dividends to the city for the career of each officer. Compared to a $2,000,000-plus investment for a one week mission, financially and statistically, the most effective choice is clear.

In another example, the Drug Enforcement Administration was hot on the trail of a multi-million dollar street gang known as the "Black Mafia Family." Agents spent years conducting surveillance, gathering intelligence, and tapping phones but constantly faced dead ends in making any detrimental in-roads to the operations core. That is, until one deputy in central Missouri was conducting his daily interdiction duties in 2004.

This deputy's Sheriff's Department assigned him to conduct full-time criminal interception on their main thoroughfare. During the stop of a vehicle that piqued his interest, he began to investigate the driver's activities further and engaged the man in some additional conversation.

After establishing sufficient suspicion, he conducted a consensual road-side search of the vehicle. After a short inspection of the contents, this small Missouri county deputy pulled 100 kilograms (that's 220 lbs) of cocaine from the car.

The perpetrator was Jabari Hayes, a key player in the Black Mafia Family. Prompted by impending criminal punishment, Jabari ultimately provided crucial information that lead to the collapse of the entire organization.

From a policing perspective, the relentless efforts of a few well-trained and dedicated patrolmen on our streets intercepted more lethal contraband on routine patrol in a shorter time than numerous agents assigned to a drug detection unit conducting in-depth, long-term investigations.

From an administrative perspective, one officer at a time serving in the course of an 8 to 12 hour shift intercepted an equivalent or larger amount of contraband than a conglomerate of detectives generating thousands of man hours and exhausting expensive investigative resources. To which resource would you prefer your tax dollars be directed and which do you believe better serves to intercept the deadly narcotics that ravage our communities every day?

Investigative units serve a purpose. Much like in the Missouri encounter, once the interdictors make the substantial seizure, then it is the detectives' turn to carry the ball forward and work to dismantle the organization responsible for the delivery. Investigators working in support of, and in concert with these criminal patrollers have been able to indict and dismantle gang and cartel leaders from a single traffic stop on a myriad of occasions, a la, Joe David's initial breakthrough netting a Medilliń Lieutenant.

Career advancement opportunities based on performance evaluations and their inherent desire to comply with supervisor directives shape the American police officer's daily activities. If emphasis is placed on traffic enforcement at one agency, then the radar guns will be kept finely tuned. If gang activity is the emphasis for another, then officers will seek out those known to be affiliated with those groups.

However, narcotic enforcement can be the underlying emphasis of any initiative. While drug detection may be most effective in gang enforcement, the traffic cop, who comes into contact with numerous motorists on a daily basis, has a high probability of coming into contact with a contraband trafficker merely as a result of their prevalence.

All officers' drug radars should be keyed in, and finely tuned by repetitive and relevant training and focus. As reflected in some officer's responses to the final question in the local survey cited in the "Police Numbers" chapter, all officers should have an understanding of the dramatic impact that drugs have on all crime. The statistic: "87%" should ring in their minds each day as they take the streets.

MIKE LEWIS

*"The credit belongs to the man who is actually in the arena;
whose face is marred by dust and sweat and blood; who
strives valiantly, who errs and comes short again and again;
who knows the great enthusiasm, the great devotions, and
spends himself in a worthy cause; who, at best, knows in
the end the triumph of high achievement and who, at worst,
if he fails, at least fails while daring greatly, so that his place
will never be with those cold and timid souls who know
neither victory nor defeat."*

-Theodore Roosevelt

In the profession of prevalence and attention to
interstate routes, historically, State Police Troopers

have been positioned to encounter vagabonds from all walks of life as they monitor cross country arteries. A small faction of troopers in our nation subscribe themselves to that "3%'er" group that actively seek out the smugglers that pass under our noses every day; an even smaller minority than those 5%'ers assigned to street level investigation groups. These men and women are the result of inspiration provided by pioneers like Joe David and our next forefather, Mike Lewis.

In 1984, Mike was hired by the Maryland State Police. He began his career much like Joe, assuming the traditional patrol functions of a state highway trooper; chasing down speeders, writing crash reports, and checking on disabled motorists.

Mike began noticing some success that other troopers were having intercepting large loads of the 1980's notorious killer, crack cocaine, on the nearby interstate that cut through Maryland, between New York City and New Jersey. Mike took note and began soliciting some insight from them on the criminal profiles they were observing.

Although he was not assigned to work on the interstate, he still patrolled a highway that linked New York City to many points south. Trooper Lewis believed attention should be paid to these back roads as they may have been serving as a route to circumvent the high profile interstate.

His drives were akin to Joe David's, in that he saw bulk drug interception as the primary weapon for stifling local and national crime. Mike realized every time he responded to a call for service; whether it was a burglary, armed robbery, or fatal car accident, illicit drugs were typically the cause of the problem.

Therefore, Mike plugged in some of those interstate tactics and began his own relentless pursuit in the war on crack cocaine. *One man . . . one uniform . . . one patrol car.*

In the years that followed, Mike proceeded to punish crack cocaine runners that traversed his patrol area. He individually executed nationally-recognized crack cocaine seizures in 1994, 1995, and 1996 on drug traffickers passing through his area.

Mike Lewis with a record drug money seizure

After Mike consistently struck powerful blows to traffickers passing through his patrol area, he was promoted to the rank of Sergeant and assigned to lead the Maryland State Police Interstate Criminal Enforcement (ICE) Team. Under Sgt Lewis' direction, the team's tenacity flourished and more record-setting encounters occurred.

The significance of the patrol tactics employed by this group in impacting all crime was well supported when Trooper Jacob Cameron of Mike's team solved a double homicide during a single traffic stop. While speaking with the driver of a vehicle he detained for a minor violation, several indicators arose that signaled Trooper Cameron and his assisting troopers to press further. Ultimately, the trunk was opened and the patrolmen were staring at two badly butchered bodies, wrapped in plastic, and being transported to New York for identification and bounty money award.

The unrelenting pursuit and many successes of Mike and his Troopers in criminal interception were not without sacrifice. Maryland State Police Trooper First Class Eddie Plank was a long time friend, colleague, and partner of Trooper Lewis. The pair netted significant drug and drug money seizures while paired together and shared the same strong-bonding drives in crushing the drug flow through their state.

Trooper Plank had just transferred from the highway corridor that Mike and he shared for several years to a patrol district covering the area of Maryland where he was born and raised. For many police officers, a great pride is felt in serving their childhood community. Highway patrolmen are often initially assigned to regions far from their home towns and they must wait for an adequate amount of seniority to select their preferred area of service.

This was a homecoming for Eddie, and he would employ the same techniques that Mike relied on and shared with him, to serve his home town.

In the first few weeks, Trooper Plank was assigned to work with rookie Trooper Dennis Lord. On October 17th, 1995, Eddie and Dennis set a speed trap along one of the state's notorious trafficking routes. Eddie would be operating the radar gun, while Trooper Lord would be pulling over the violators. After a few minutes of waiting, they had the first fish in the net and Eddie was radioing to the rookie for the car to be stopped.

While the new trooper was conducting his enforcement action, another car came through at a high rate of speed. Eddie pulled from his position and chased it down. During his initial contact with the driver and passenger, Eddie noticed a few of those trainable indicators that signaled the men in the car were up to no good.

Eddie radioed for his rookie companion to join him, so he could investigate further. When Trooper Lord arrived and he briefed him of his suspicions, Eddie approached the driver's door of the stopped car for the second time and asked the driver to come out of the car. As the driver reached for the door handle, he simultaneously reached for a pistol.

The man motioned to open the door, but instead, shot Trooper Plank in the face, killing him instantly.

As the vehicle sped away, Trooper Lord began firing at the vehicle. One of the occupants was shot in the head and these violent criminals were later apprehended after a short man hunt. They were also found to be transporting almost one pound of crack cocaine in the car at the time of the shooting.

Despite the apprehension and seizure, the loss to Mike and the law enforcement community was catastrophic. Mike had lost a dear friend and a family had lost a husband and father, who made the ultimate sacrifice for the cause Mike and he had cared for so deeply.

Some may think, "What a waste to lose the life of a productive member of society, all over some dope" or "Drugs are a victimless crime, why do the police put themselves in harm's way, just to stop trafficking?". But these patrolmen see that narcotic offenses are not victimless. They see the crimes, violent and otherwise, spawned by the use and delivery of all brands of illicit drugs. They understand that heroically laying it all on the line for the purpose of drug interception is the essence of their oath to serve and protect.

We should think about how many lives Trooper Plank may have saved that day in giving his own. Cocaine, let alone crack cocaine, is a destructive drug that ravages families, jobs, and the human body. By the seizure of drugs that day, hundreds of lives were directly affected and potentially saved by the selfless vigilance of Trooper Plank.

Mike is and was a Trooper (in every sense of the word) and realized the best and only way to pay homage to his fallen brother was to continue to press the fight.

Thirteen weeks after Eddie's murder, Mike found himself in a battle for his own life during a similar encounter. After making a traffic stop on a motorist who set off his alarm bells, Mike began looking into things a bit further. Trooper Lewis gained consent from the driver to search and subsequently found some contraband in the car. When Mike went to make the apprehension, the fight was on. Trooper Lewis was by himself with a man who had nothing to lose and was grappling for the patrolman's gun.

As the hand-to-hand battle raged on, the trafficker broke away and re-entered his vehicle. In a moment of desperation, the offender—who had already shown the desire to use deadly force against the

Trooper—put his car in drive and attempted to run over Mike. In return, Mike was forced to fire three shots into the vehicle, ultimately killing his foe.

Faced with a life-threatening occurrence in a time when the cold-blooded killing of his dear friend was so fresh in his mind, Mike was able to rage on, and win the battle. His display of the warrior spirit shined brightly that day, as it had done so many times before and so many times from thereon.

As a matter of departmental procedure, Mike was taken to a local hospital following the confrontation for physical and psychological evaluation. Mike's lovely wife met him there and during the long wait of a typical hospital emergency room, she strongly encouraged him to reconsider his career path. Mike simply pacified his concerned wife by saying, "we'll talk about that later".

Despite Mrs. Lewis' urgings, Mike returned to work two weeks later and quickly found himself in pursuit of another drug trafficker during his first night back on patrol. This high speed chase ended with the safe capture of the fleeing criminal and the narcotics he was attempting to transport across state lines.

Mike was right back in the saddle and, to the benefit of our nation, he did not reconsider his career path (and yes, Mr and Mrs Lewis are still married after 29 years together). Mike and his wife recognized his work as his calling and knew that it was unequivocally important to the safety and security of their community, state, and country.

After taking hundreds of pounds of illicit drugs out of his community, losing a friend, having to kill a criminal to save his own life, and dodging two separate bounties on his head posted by narco-terrorist groups, Mike retired from the Maryland State Police in 2006. He subsequently ran for Sheriff in a Maryland county and was elected by a land slide. Mike's work to eradicate drugs from the eastern coast of the U.S. was well publicized and the citizens of his county rewarded him for his labor.

Mike continues to serve as Sheriff, and has passed on his techniques to all of the deputies who serve his community. Now, his agency funds its specialized services through intercepted drug money found passing into or through the county. Mike is another fine example of a pioneer who has applied these tactics successfully and attained financial independence for his agency, enhanced public service to his community, and annually saves hundreds of thousands of his citizen's tax dollars. Sheriff Lewis is the administrative role model for this newly evolving counter-drug strategy. His bewildering achievements as a state patrolmen and his leadership as a Sheriff have positioned him as one of our country's cornerstones of success in the War on Drugs.

Mike also travels the country and the world (to include Australia, London, Germany, Russia, and the West Indies), teaching classes to police officers on these tactics and the examples of the fruits of their application. He also designed a seminar for police administrators, to share the importance and potential of this cause, as well as passing on his imperial mission: the refusal to surrender to drug traffickers and engagement of *every* patrol officer in the realization that drug interception is their responsibility.

Know Your Enemy . . .

*"When bad men combine, the good must associate else
they will fall one by one, an unpitied sacrifice in a
contemptible struggle."*

-Edmund Burke

Sun Tzu said, "If ignorant both of your enemy and
yourself, you are certain to be in peril." Assessing
how well we understand "ourselves" (meaning our
police forces in this interpretation) is answered by
our failure to involve almost 95% of our personnel to
the most identifiable cause of crime, as well as the
potential source for monumental asset and currency
apprehension.

Based on this fact, one could argue that we would
be in Sun Tzu's "peril" category based on our
"knowledge" of and response to the principle cause
of crime in our nation. So how do we begin to identify
and know our enemy? Certainly an opponent this
calculating and effective must be rather difficult to
detect.

On the contrary; as our first two forefathers have
proven, narco-terrorists have few basic, identifiable
methods in contraband delivery to the United States.
In the US federal indictment of one trafficking
organization, the investigators describe the means

of drug transportation as the following (but not limited to): Boeing 747 cargo aircraft, private aircraft, submarines and other submersible vessels, container ships, go-fast boats, fishing vessels, buses, rail cars, tractor trailers, and automobiles[xvi].

Essentially, until teleportation becomes available to the drug trafficker, these smuggling methods will continue to be a mainstay of their industry. Coincidentally, criminals are most susceptible to apprehension while in the act of smuggling.

For the integrity and confidentiality of these newly evolving police tactics, the methods and profiles of contraband smugglers will not be discussed at any point. It is important, however, to define the overall root of our drug flow, as well as how we, as a nation, have means of evening the score in the drug war, while bringing strong financial and social benefits to our nation.

The fertile terrain and climates of Columbia, Bolivia, and Peru have long been acknowledged as the home of the coca plant. As demand grows, the fields of South and Central America have turned to producing mass quantities of poppies, ergo, a heroin onslaught like America has never seen before. Clandestine drug labs in Central America are churning out Crystal Methamphetamine in bulk. The open sea ports of South American countries allow for the unobstructed export of bumper crops of deadly, crime causing drugs to ports in Central America.

As with all manufacturing and agriculture, a strong logistics entity is required to bring the product to the end-user. Enter the cartels of Mexico. When examining the physicality of the country on a map, a funnel shape is a geographically and analogically

66

appropriate description. Narrowed end at the portal to the Central Americas; wide end opening to the vast borders of the United States, into the arms of the lucrative drug demand.

The Mexican Cartels have turned the country into a functional conduit of illicit narcotics from the south, through their packaging and transportation schemes, then across the border and on to their logistics agents positioned in cities across the United States. From those American cities, the agents will divide the shipments and disperse them to a pyramid of street dealers.

The passage of the North American Free Trade Agreement in 1994, and the associated loosening of border passages, in the interest of commerce has allowed for a more brazened approach to smuggling. Considering the sheer volume of traffic thrown at Border agents on a daily basis, crossing under the guise of US/Mexico business transportation or personal travel has become drastically easier.

Once a drug shipment clears the border, it will typically move to a nearby distribution point. From there, it is fanned throughout the country on our highways and bi-ways, ultimately arriving at local distribution centers. While the appearance of these centers often dramatically differs from those of legitimate commerce, the process is the same. From this point, the high level street dealers are supplied with varying quantities and forms of bulk narcotic for disbursement among their chains of lower level dealers.

Generally, here enters local law enforcement. So much emphasis of the police assigned to investigating drug crimes is placed on street level dealers. From state police driven task forces, to county or city metro narcotic units; undercover hand-to-hand busts and search warrants on crack houses are executed in effort to stem drug activity in our communities.

Analogically speaking, this method is akin to kicking aside a well-shaped chunk of cork while using a small bucket to bail out your boat that is rapidly filling with water. Why not pick up that cork and plug the hole, completely?

We know the primary and sometimes the sole source of drug flow (our boat's water leak) into our communities. We also know the general destination of the currency as it flows from our cities, states, and country.

Local law enforcement (our cork) has numerous resources and training grounds for tracking and identifying the source of our crime-creator, such as the aforementioned Desert Snow. Police agencies have the assets to begin a true battle with every serving uniformed and non-uniformed police officer. All it requires is basic, consistent, continued training, intertwined with vigilance, and direction.

ROBBIE BISHOP, THE CAREER

"Born on a mountain top in Tennessee,
Greenest state in the land of the free.
Raised in the woods so's he knew every tree,
Killed him a bear when he was only three.

Davy, Davy Crockett King, of the Wild Frontier.

Fought single handed through the Injun war,
Till the Creeks was whipped and peace was restored.
And while he was handling this risky chore,
Made himself a legend, forevermore.

Davy, Davy Crockett, the man who don't know fear . . ."

Perhaps the last quote you thought you would read in a non-fiction compilation is the tune of a folklore hero. However, Davy's introductory song is quite appropriate, as it runs parallel to the life of our third forefather in this crusade.

Robbie Bishop was born and raised in the mountain country along the Georgia/Tennessee border. Just like Davy, he was an outdoor adventurer, always testing the limits of his courage and skill. When Robbie was of age, he continued his passion for exploration and joined the Marine Corp to fulfill his urge to serve and prepare himself for life.

When Robbie exited the Corp, he already had his career of choice in mind. For this southern serviceman, a return to his homeland to act as a protector of the people was a natural fit.

Unknown to Robbie at the on-set of his police profession, the southeastern region of the United States allowed for a peaceful operations center for international drug cartels, as well as rarely patrolled thoroughfares for drug runners zooming up and down the east coast. This area was far from the hustle and bustle of urban sprawls and the watchful eyes of border patrol agents in the southwest.

Police in the region were either traditional urban cops, dealing with daily street crimes; or rough and tumble county Sheriff's deputies (with little police training or experience), who dealt with the occasional live-stock in the highway or back-road domestic disputes.

Robbie started his police career as a Sheriff's Deputy in rural northern Georgia in 1985. Robbie's inauguration ran a similar course of other major criminal interceptors of his time. His typical law enforcement duties were regimented to routine calls for service, traffic enforcement, and community policing.

Robbie's life did benefit from these occasionally mundane traditional police roles. While instructing citizens during a community neighborhood watch meeting, he met the acquaintance of his wife-to-be.

Lisa Bishop recalls of her "Type-A" personality husband that when Robbie saw something he wanted, he went out and got it. Lisa, who attended the meeting with her boyfriend at the time, learned through the grapevine shortly afterward that Robbie was interested in her and was pressing for a date.

Lisa's relationship with her boyfriend ended and soon Robbie's goal was attained. Three months later, they were engaged. Marriage followed several months after that.

Robbie's determination applied to all facets of his life, to include his work ethic. Lisa would come to provide the ever important personal support structure for Robbie to thrive professionally. As the saying goes; "behind every great man is a great woman".

While employed by a local Sheriff's Department in northern Georgia, Robbie was assigned to a drug enforcement unit in 1989 and began working undercover for the first time. Robbie was immediately attracted to the thrill of drug detection, and the reading of people's actions and body language.

After a two year stint in this role, Robbie realized his place was on the street, patrolling for the people. He found that he could make the most impact on crime in that role.

Unfortunately for the community Robbie served, the Sheriff did not want Robbie to return to a patrol function and insisted he continue serving in the narrow-scoped function of the drug group.

Robbie, who was always pressing forward, never letting the grass grow under his feet, left this office and transferred to a nearby Sheriff's Department north of Atlanta, where he served as a drug-sniffing dog handler.

It was at this new office where Robbie began to commingle his love for drug trafficker apprehension with aggressive patrol work on major thoroughfares. Not only did he become a "DUI" champion, Robbie was quickly attaining national law enforcement recognition for making sizable drug and drug money seizures in his region. While these apprehensions left a positive impact on society, Robbie recognized that the traffickers he was encountering were lower level gang members, and street dealers bleeding out the drugs from the major hub of Atlanta, to points north. He wanted to strike out at a higher level of smuggler.

Like a Harvard graduate pushing for vertical advancement in the business world, this experienced and upwardly mobile patrolman with a highly marketable skill-set was on the prowl for the next agency to facilitate his drives and promote his growth. With his rapidly increasing notoriety, he was recruited by a Sheriff's Department about two hours south of Atlanta. This opportunity would put him in the crux of the inbound metropolitan dope traffic. With Lisa's support, Robbie shifted to the new agency and faced a two hour commute (one way) to perform the job he loved and apply the techniques he was mastering.

Robbie's forecast of the drug activity passing through this new region was precise. Robbie was executing unprecedented apprehensions of illicit narcotics along this corridor. During one traffic stop in Robbie's new hunting ground, his ability to sift through cover stories and innocent facades resulted in the seizure of 85 kilograms of cocaine.

That's 85,000 grams or 187 pounds of dangerous narcotic that would have hit the streets and spread like cockroaches, with each gram opening its own Pandora's box of associated crime and crushed lives. Seizures of this nature were and are of epic proportion in law enforcement. Agents working in drug detection task forces can work for years in this assignment without ever seeing a tiny fraction of this amount of narcotics.

Robbie's 85 kilogram cocaine seizure

Agency support is an integral part in the success of these aggressive criminal enforcement techniques. Despite some incredible results, Robbie became disenchanted with the administrative demeanor of this agency and moved on to the next patrol venue.

In the new theatre at the Georgia/Florida border, Robbie was monitoring the paths that traversed directly from the Floridian ports to the hub of Atlanta. Colossal loads of drugs north bound and buckets of drug money south bound.

Robbie positioned himself to monitor traffic on one such southerly route, one particular afternoon. A van passed by and, based on a few indicators, Robbie decided the vehicle deserved a second look.

It takes a trained and experienced eye like Robbie's to discern within seconds of the initial conversation with the driver and passengers that nefarious activity was occurring within that vehicle. Not only did Robbie's red flags fly while speaking with the occupants, he almost immediately noticed the false compartment built into the van's interior.

After safely detaining the travelers, Robbie cracked opened the metal-capped, carpet covered alcove to reveal bundles of United States currency. Robbie began pulling the plastic-wrapped stacks of bills from the hiding place and stacking them on top of one, another.

As the pile grew taller and Robbie reached deeper in the crevice, it seemed impossible that he could pull out another package. However, this was a world class interdictor, who was positioned to make the largest impact on American crime and just like all of his other encounters, the possibilities were endless.

At the end of the day, Robbie executed the largest money seizure of his prosperous career. The outwardly unassuming Florida-bound van tooling down the road contained over $900,000 in United States currency. Under statutory regulations,

Robbie's employer would split the award with the State of Georgia, and incorporate the funds into its budget to better service the community and off-set the citizen's tax dollars.

In this fertile interception zone, Deputy Bishop continued stopping gigantic shipments of drugs en route to urban distribution points and loads of cash traveling back to the southern sources. Incidentally, he was also five hours away from Lisa.

Despite the distant separation, Robbie continued to thrive due to the support he received. Robbie's employer provided him with a patrol vehicle to make the ten hour drive (roundtrip) to visit his family on the weekend and they paid his $600 per month cell phone bill to help keep him in touch with his loved ones, as well.

From his wife; he was provided understanding. Lisa held a strong appreciation for Robbie's intense drive and commitment to this vitally important cause.

Robbie never wasted an opportunity, and used his experiences from the various agencies he served to expand his network and establish training programs for police officers from across the region. Not having the highest business acumen, Robbie's mission in spreading his gospel was nondiscriminatory.

Robbie would travel for hours, just to teach a small class on this specific criminal patrol tactic in an old, rusted-out trailer, where the students and even the teacher would occasionally fall through the floor of the structure due to the dilapidated conditions. For Robbie, the venue and the instructor pay was never important. It was all about the message and the preaching.

Lisa recalls that Robbie was as excited as a child on his birthday with each and every one of his apprehensions. He was equally excited by seizures made by his peers and students. For Robbie, it was a means for making a national impact on crime.

While Robbie was serving the south and spreading his message, Lisa faced a tragedy in the loss of her brother in a car accident. Robbie could no longer compromise the closeness with Lisa and his children, and he returned home to reciprocate the long-standing support she had showed him.

However, one of our nation's most formidable forces against crime would not be pulled from his watch for long.

THE GLOBAL WAR ON TERROR

*"When the will defies fear, when duty throws the gauntlet
down to fate, when honor scorns to compromise with death
—that is heroism."*

Robert Green Ingersoll

On September 9th, 2001, Maryland State Police
Trooper Joseph Catalano stopped Ziad Jarrah for
driving his rental car at 90 mph in a 65 mph zone on
Interstate 95 through the northern part of the state.
Trooper Catalano did not receive any information
about Jarrah when he checked his name through
computer databases, nor did he detect any indicators
from the man to pique the Trooper's curiosity about
his activity.

As another contributing factor to Jarrah's ultimate
release from the traffic stop, Maryland State
Police Troopers were under scrutiny at the time for
conducting searches on people of color, probable
cause or not; lessening the Trooper's desire to
investigate further.

Trooper Catalano wrote Jarrah the $270 traffic ticket
and released him from the stop. Less than two days
later, Ziad Jarrah highjacked United flight 93, that

crashed into a field near Shanksville, Pa, killing everyone on board.

At any time prior to the morning of September 11th, 2001, if Trooper Catalano or any other American patrolman had encountered Jarrah or one of his associates passing through their community and had cause to search the man or his vehicle, they still would most-likely not have made much of a few flight manuals and a set of box cutters in his possession.

It was only after the rental vehicle borrowed by Jarrah was located at the Newark, New Jersey airport, did federal agents discover the ticket Trooper Catalano issued to Jarrah and retraced the steps to the Maryland State Police contact.

––––––––––

The date was April 19th, 1995, on a typically quiet and unassuming highway in rural Oklahoma. A state trooper was solemnly going about his patrol duties after leaving his office where the television was broadcasting live reports from the destruction of the Murrah Federal Building in the heart of the heartland. Trooper Charlie Hanger stopped to help a couple of ladies who had the misfortune of a broken down car. After calling a tow truck for the stranded motorists, he began pulling away.

Just like any good patrolman, he was constantly aware of his surroundings and took note of a yellow Mercury that passed by him and the disabled vehicle.

Trooper Hanger continued in the same direction as the coupe. As he rolled up behind it, he noticed the car did not have any license plates. He recognized that the lack of registration may be the indication of a stolen car and decided it was time to take some enforcement action.

Charlie switched on his overhead lights and brought the unregistered car to the curb. As he summoned the driver out of the car to speak with him, Trooper Hanger noticed a bulge in his pocket. He reasoned the man may have a gun concealed on him, and after some initial questioning from the other side of the Trooper's pistol, the man confessed he did, indeed, have a firearm in his waistband (a violation of Oklahoma law and a severe concern for any officer's safety).

Acting quickly and alone, Trooper Hanger took the driver, Timothy James McVeigh, into custody. After detaining McVeigh at the nearby jail, Trooper Hanger learned the FBI was looking to speak with him after finding connections to this domestic terrorist near the crime scene in Oklahoma City.

His state just faced arguably the most horrific disaster it had ever faced and, hopefully, will ever have to face. But Trooper Hanger knew his responsibility to his citizens was not to sit and stare at the tragedy on television. It was to get out on the road and uphold the high standards of his profession. In doing so, he brought one of the most violent terrorists in American history to justice. And he did this by applying constant vigilance and basic, trainable, criminal detection techniques.

In a speech to a community meeting in 1999, Trooper (retired) Hanger told the crowd, "Alert officers all over our communities and our highways are stopping these criminals by being there. I don't hold the patent on it—I was in the right spot at the right time . . ."

No one could have said it better, and no other incident can better capture the upmost importance of criminal interception techniques than Charlie's demonstration that solemn April morning.

Post 09/11, communication and intelligence of security threats have dramatically increased on all levels, from the average citizen to the Commander-in-Chief. Americans are briefed frequently on terrorist threats, reported activities, and the related "threat level" as audited by the Department of Homeland Security.

The FBI and CIA have worked diligently on an international level, curbing numerous would-be attacks, and coordinating military operations to strike out at the threat sources abroad. American police officers also receive frequent updates about alleged terrorist activities. The reports are rather general in nature and rarely define any specific threat. In summary, the emphasis is usually on vigilance.

As evidenced by the Oklahoma Highway Patrol and Maryland State Police stops, our American patrolmen's pro-activity and constant contact with the public results in their highest probability of criminal interception. If all US police forces were provided the appropriate training, given the administrative support, and put to task knowing that all of the resources were in place for successful major criminal apprehension, then agency liability is dramatically reduced and bad people are more frequently removed from the streets.

We not only owe it to our police to direct them on this path armed with the appropriate sword and shield, but we also owe it to our own livelihood, well-being, and security.

Fortunately, numerous law enforcement agencies across the United States have recognized the importance of these detection techniques, and have supplied at least a portion of their patrolmen with these apprehension tools. Joe David's Desert Snow organization, whose emphasis focuses on the seizure of bulk shipments of drugs and money, tracked the apprehension of terrorists and explosives by Desert Snow trainees who were applying the organization's tactics during routine patrol. From 2005 to 2010, these select few interceptors initiated 33 cases involving the seizure of explosive devices and captured 56 suspected terrorists in the process[xvii].

To reiterate: these apprehensions were made by the (less than) 3% of all patrolman who were trained in criminal interception. These patrolmen are the uniformed front lines of all of our communities, not federal agents with exemplary resources. Not only are these men and women making their towns, counties, and states a safer place by eradicating bulk amounts of dangerous drugs and enhancing public safety, they are saving millions of tax dollars by seizing narcotic funds to be put to use by their agency. They are also impeding international terrorist activity as a result of their attention to detail and duty. And all of these tactics are trainable to all of our policemen. The resources are already in place, the education is available.

THE CORRIDORS

"We all dream of a world full of sunshine, happiness and peace. The problem is half the people think it sounds like a wonderful place to live in. The other half thinks it sounds like a wonderful place to pillage."

-HG Duncan, USMC (ret.)

As I examined the reports on mass amounts of drugs and drug money circulating through my region of the country, I looked to a road map to see the probable routes that those narcotics followed as they ultimately bled onto my streets. Once I knew my enemy (or understood the source of these issues), it was easy to trace the route with my index finger from the south, straight up to the Windy City. I was studying the same road maps in the same manner that so many drug mules had done before.

During the course of my research, I relied heavily on publicly available data published on federal government web sites. I was surprised to find a blatantly defined drug corridor map plotted out in one drug administration's study posted on their website. And there-one of eight highlighted paths-was "Corridor F." Basically, the same route I had traced with my index finger. The identification of these influx routes seemed all too easy.

So why weren't we *all* doing what the "pioneers" taught us to do? Why were we all not constantly monitoring these routes and intercepting shipments in either direction?

I set out to find the answer from four different law enforcement agencies along Corridor F who support the cause of major criminal interception and are surrounded by other agencies that do not.

Could it really be so fruitful that small blocs of law enforcement were dedicating full-time resources to this type of patrol? Were agencies really generating enough revenue (to the tune of hundreds of thousands of dollars) to support entire divisions of their department? And were these "units" just fly-by-night operations with hit-or-miss success?

What I found along the way was astonishing dedication, intensity, and solid bottom-line results. The men and women of these police agencies were proving that those trainable tactics were the most productive tools in fighting crime and generating revenue, not just in their region, but in the entire nation.

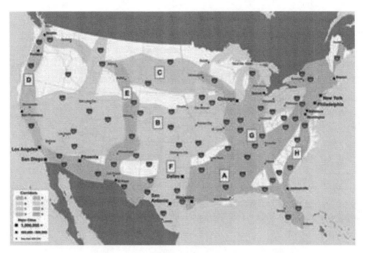

National Drug Control Strategy 2010
Map of Drug Smuggling Corridors

CORRIDOR F, SECTION A: TEXAS

*"Texas has yet to learn submission to any oppression,
come from what source it may"*

-Sam Houston

As I geared up the car and headed out of the garage at 3 am for my cross country venture, I had visions about what Texas would look like. Having never visited the state (much less the two other states I would be passing through: Missouri and Oklahoma), all I knew was that everything was "bigger in Texas." Based on the size of the drug loads and money seizures I was seeing Texas local law enforcement posting on the Desert Snow website, it seemed at least that much was true.

With the Lone Star State holding the lion's share of the US/Mexico border (1,254 of 1,969 miles) the probability of Texas patrolman encountering traffickers making a run north was relatively high. Geographically and evidentially speaking, this was a fantastic starting point for my tour.

As the 14 hour drive from home came to a close and I broached the Texas-Oklahoma border, the terrain seemed to break open into a kind of territory that I had never before seen. With regions of rolling and often cavernous hills and valleys next to road signs cautioning of gusty winds in excess of 100 mph, it struck mental images of another territory I also have yet to visit . . . the moon.

The fruitful plains of the state spread open as I rolled west from the jagged hill country. Everything truly was bigger here. From horizon to horizon, the sky was richer and deeper. The open fields seemed to stretch to the ends of the earth with no obstruction. Even the cattle grazing the fields were dominatingly larger than the cows of the Illinois prairie.

This was a portrait of the Wild West, where cowboys roamed the fields chasing down stray herds, and living by the law of the land. However, it was not the 1800's. It was the new millennium, and those men in cowboy hats were the lawmen of the Texas Highway Patrol. Working by the mantra of their superiors, they dedicate their service to "catching bad people doing bad things." These men arduously work the highways and bi-ways that are the birth of the drug in-flux to the United States.

I had the fortunate opportunity of dropping in on one patrol post, whose troopers notch grandiose seizures of drug shipments passing through the state to all points east and north. This particular division of the Highway Patrol is at the apex of narco-trafficking from the southwestern region of the country. Working such a fertile region nets the group annual cash seizures in the ball park of three to four million dollars.

By Texas statute, once the necessary court proceedings are brought to a close, the highway patrol is awarded eighty percent of the funds (and like most other state and federal procedures, the other twenty percent is vested in the seizure counsel, i.e. district attorney, state's attorney, etc). The work of this particular patrol post is the bread and butter that has provided for a new firearms training range and a myriad of equipment for troopers across the state.

Naturally, I assumed the work of these patrolmen mirrored the tasks of other Troopers in the state, especially those directly along the US/Mexico border. However, in consistency with national statistics, only a small percentage of Troopers are assigned to seek out these most-critical offenders. According to some troopers, many others simply are not interested in this type of criminal patrol.

Even within this unit, the majority of patrolmen are assigned to routine calls for service and basic traffic enforcement on state routes. When time allows, they take the opportunity to sneak out, and make the encounters that truly make an impact. One trooper from this post on one such venture (by following those basic trainable techniques) intercepted a man trafficking over 600 illegal rifles across the country. The same trooper routinely lays claim to multiple pounds of deadly crystal meth making its way north and east.

Whether you live in Illinois, Texas, Florida or any another state in the US, the impact that these few men from one patrol post have on the source of 87% of the crime that rattles our foundation on a daily basis is of national importance.

When I asked one trooper (who dedicates his career to seeking and destroying these terrorists) what drives his unrelenting pursuit, he paused, gazed down at his desk to a family photo of his daughters, then pointed to it and simply stated, "those girls."

His realization that his work had local, regional, and national impact on murderous criminal activity was strongly driven by the power of a father's love for his children and for his desire to make this a better world for them. On principle alone, few other causes are as personal and righteous for any human being.

ROBBIE BISHOP, THE DESTINY

"When young men seek to be like you,

When powerful men look over their shoulder at you,

When cowardly men plot behind your back,

And evil men want you dead . . .

Only then will you have done your share."

~Phil Messina

After returning home to tend to his wife Lisa in her time of crisis, Robbie's type-A drive was pushing him back onto the streets. Every second he was off the road, lead to another minute for a drug mule to slide into their destination, undetected.

Robbie's internal drives were not the long factor in his quick return to patrol. Robbie was a legend of his time and recruitment of his skills were heavy in the South East. A DEA agent, who was a friend of Robbie's, had pointed him toward a small community, after hearing the police department wanted to start up a criminal interception program.

Seeking to expand his impact, Robbie took the direction of his federal friend and keyed in on a portion of Georgia he had not yet worked. The small town of Villa Rica, located west of Atlanta, was about to be graced by the terminator of drug trafficking.

Robbie went to work in Villa Rica in September of 1996, and worked his first six weeks for free. Robbie believed so strongly in the importance of this cause he was willing to donate his time to show the town what he was capable of accomplishing. Robbie worked tirelessly everyday because (as he would say) people wanted to see what he could do, not what he had done.

This pioneer was often challenged by small town councils and police administrations about the importance of stopping large drug loads as they pass through (and not stop in) their communities. Most would not understand the justification of posting a patrolman on the thoroughfares, when their resources were few and police patrols were expected on the village streets. Robbie reasoned with them that the big loads may not be stopping in their town, but it was heading to the urban hub, where it would be stripped down and brought back by local traffickers and their citizens.

Robbie would question, "When these activities are legally detectable, why not stop it at the source, cutting off the head of the snake?" He often used the "Wal-Mart" analogy, referring to the drug cartels logistical methods mirroring that of traditional corporate distributors. Shipments are brought into a hub, broken down, and then sent back out into the community storefronts. The drug trade is no different.

Along with the bulk shipments of narcotics that Robbie seized, also came the bulk shipments of narcotics money. If the drug deterrence that created so many debilitating secondary crimes did not sway the minds of his critics, Robbie's demonstration of the substantial monetary proceeds an agency could achieve through the forfeiture of a trafficker's proceeds would usually push the department-heads into the light.

Not surprisingly, Robbie learned that the west side of Atlanta presented similar opportunities as the points north and south that founded his career. Soon, he was back in the routine of creating dramatic *in-roads* to stopping illicit drug influx. Robbie brought his usual habits of relentlessly long work hours (fourteen to sixteen at a time) and ordering pizza delivery on the highway so he could maintain surveillance of his domain to maximize interception success.

During Robbie's domain over the Interstate 20 corridor, he set records in seizures from truckers attempting to smuggle dope into the big city to the east. In a ten day period, Robbie stopped five semis, and seized the following amounts of marijuana: 2,105 pounds, 75 pounds, 1,500 pounds, 1,000 pounds, 750 pounds grouped with 3 kilograms of cocaine. Oh yeah, the one-time head of the Gulf Cartel, one of Mexico's most murderous mafias, was along for the ride on one of the seizures, as well.

Robbie with another record cash seizure

Robbie's fame in the police and citizen communities was destined to be shared in the criminal community as well. Criminal organizations' survival instincts force them to adapt to a threat to their existence and use whatever means necessary to eliminate that threat and secure their position. If anyone was ever a threat to the criminal world, it would be our three forefathers of criminal patrol. In this instance, it was Robbie Edward Bishop.

On January 20th, 1999, Robbie was monitoring traffic on a Villa Rica thoroughfare when a passing vehicle caught his eye. Robbie chased down the car, which was occupied by a man traveling alone, on his way west from Atlanta.

It is unclear exactly what transpired between the time of the stop and the first passing motorist's discovery, but Robbie was gunned down on the side of the road, doing what he had dedicated his life to do.

Crime scene analysis indicated that Robbie and the driver were meeting in between their respective vehicles. It appeared that Robbie turned away from the man to reach through his squad car's open driver's window and set down his ticket book, when the violent criminal opened fire as he approached Robbie.

Captain Bishop never had an opportunity to fight back.

Some theorized that Robbie's assassination was a carefully plotted operation. However, the down fall of this policing titan came at the hands of a meaningless thug. He was a desperate man, who simply did not want to return to jail, so he attacked Robbie in cold blood.

Robbie's probable mindset was that the man had some illegal currency in the vehicle. Robbie likely reasoned that he would seize the drug cash, give him a receipt and a court date to argue for the cash, if he so chose, and send him on his way.

Robbie's killer fled the scene in his car, ultimately dumping it and catching a flight out of town. Investigators worked feverishly to avenge this hero's death. Just a few days later, the killer was apprehended in front of a donut shop in Canada.

Ironically, the murderer was a career criminal and was reading Robbie like Robbie was reading him. His perception was that this cop was going to search him and his car, find a gun he illegally possessed, and send him back to prison . . . an option he was not willing to accept.

What this cold blooded killer failed to realize, whatever his motive, is that Robbie was already larger than life. The mission he carried out on a daily basis over the course of a decade made him immortal to law enforcement officers across the nation.

His training philosophies and criminal identification tactics were taught to a mass of pupils, and taking the man's life would only make his cause that much stronger. His death served to motivate, and mobilize thousands of officers to follow Master Bishop's footsteps in the only true war on crime.

Robbie was laid to rest on a Wednesday. The powerful training organization that was formed in his honor was founded the following Saturday. Today, the National Criminal Enforcement Association is over 4,000 members strong; and holds annual trainings and certifications, teaching officers these vitally necessary tactics that, time and time again, have proven themselves the most effective in ferreting out massive amounts of illicit drugs and awarding their agencies with millions of dollars of drug money for operations.

Robbie's disciples continue to carry on his work and we as a nation continue to reap the rewards of his campaign. While the man will always be missed, his efforts will live on forever.

As Robbie's posthumously founded organization salutes him:

"Rest in peace, Warrior, rest in peace."

Robbie Edward Bishop, 1964-1999

THE ENEMY
(CONTINUED)

"Never forget those who died. Never forget those who killed them."

-HG Duncan, USMC (ret)

It's no secret who supplies our nation with its illegal drugs. Mexican drug cartels are defined, plotted, and scorned on various American government web sites that are available to the public. Even Forbes magazine managed to glamorize one of the elite cartel kingpins. Of the eighteen to thirty-nine BILLION dollars of US currency out of circulation in foreign drug markets, ninety percent of that is in the hands of Mexican drug cartels. Eighty percent of that share is believed to be in the control of ONE MAN at the helm of that cartel.

Joaquin "El Chapo" Guzman

Forbes magazine's 2009 billionaire #701, Joaquin "El Chapo" Guzman Loera, head of the Sinaloan Cartel, is immortalized by this American publication for his fortune made on the bodies of American citizens killed by drug use and drug-related crimes. As well as the bodies of U.S. and Mexican police and federal agents killed in the war against him.

Under the heading of "Industry" in El Chapo's profile, Forbes casually notes: "shipping."[xviii]

This dismissive approach to the illegal drug sub-culture is bred from decades of desensitization to its impact on our society. Narcotic abuse has entrenched itself in our lives and, chances are, you know someone in your life who has been effected by illegal drugs.

Many have thrown up the white flag in the "war" and argue for legalization of some or most of these deadly substances. Never mind the crimes that dominate our society that are committed by people under the influence of these intoxifiers. Not to mention the billions of dollars spent in the treatment and rehabilitation of drug abusers.

Granted, smuggling has always happened and will always happen. However, there are concrete solutions to begin turning the tide and move toward winning the war. We have the ability to take specific, precise, tactical approaches to deterring criminal activity, all the while benefiting socially and financially from this underground market.

The Drug War has been a constant drain on tax-payer money and government resources since the battle broke out more than three decades ago. Perhaps it is time for us to entertain what may be called the "Nottingham" approach. This involves the ethical "robbing" of our currency from drug couriers and returning it to our community.

By employing the teaching of our forefathers across the country and turning our police forces into present-day Robin Hoods, we stand a strong chance of discontinuing the railroading, leveling the playing field, and benefiting from substantial forfeiture proceeds.

Corridor F, Section B: Oklahoma

"Resilience is woven deeply into the fabric of Oklahoma.
Throw us an obstacle and we grow stronger"

-Brad Henry

At the center of America, the heartland states serve as a conduit to the coasts for vacationers, commerce, and criminals. As evidenced by retired Trooper Charlie Hanger's apprehension of Timothy McVeigh, the cross roads of the red-dirt state are no exception.

During the course of my travels, I did not observe more police presence on the roadways in any other state than Oklahoma. On day one, as I headed west, I was surprised not to come in contact with the highway patrol by way of lights flashing in my rear view mirror. It seemed I passed a black and white every ten to fifteen minutes.

On the path northeast from the border (that so many drug traffickers have traveled before me), I linked up with an Oklahoma Trooper whose full-time assignment was aggressive criminal patrol on the state's highways. My hopes for a first hand criminal interception experience during my ride-along were high, based merely on the dramatically visible presence of uniformed patrol on the major thoroughfares.

I was fortunate to head out for a shift where our assignment was the detection of drug traffickers heading east from western source locations. The Trooper was partnered with another patrolman, and both men were armed with the essential, high quality training that is provided by Desert Snow. At $1,000 per class, agencies like this can justify the one-time initial education cost and occasional recurring training. The investment pays off when they unleash this group of fifteen patrollers on the state highways and watch them net at least ten million dollars cash, annually, (over $666,000 per trooper) for use toward protective equipment, patrol computers, and other necessary tools for the entire 800-plus trooper Highway Patrol.

From the same seizure fund, the fifteen man group is afforded new patrol cars, police dogs, and various criminal apprehension apparatus to properly execute their daily duties.

By dedicating a small portion of full-time resources to this cause, the highway patrol has demonstrated their superior ability to ferret out major criminals and their commitment to their citizens by seeking out those self-supporting illicit funds.

Geographically speaking, Oklahoma is the gateway to America for drugs entering from the south and west. This faction of troopers monitors traffic on strategic routes with constant and highly professional vigilance. Trained in the ethical tactics of criminal interception, the patrolmen's first priority is maintaining integrity of the civil expectations of everyone they encounter.

The trooper I partnered with was consistently polite, courteous, and systematic in the manner that he approached every motorist. Despite numerous contacts with people passing through his patrol region that day, we did not seize any drugs or even conduct a search of a vehicle.

Initially, my gut instinct was to be disappointed by the lack of productivity that day. I came to see these vigilant watchmen grabbing narco-terrorist after narco-terrorist, but so far: two states and no yield.

Then I remembered the essence of this labor: ethics and professionalism. With the tutoring of law enforcement's prestigious criminal interception training organizations, these small factions of police are able to discern criminal activity from normal activity with a few basic observations and non-invasive questioning. This fine line of police/ public contact promotes the civility (not just the necessity) of this line of work.

These specifically assigned Troopers are not running rogue, searching every camper and mini-van traveling to a family vacation at Yellow Stone. The finely-tuned techniques in criminal profiling maintain the constitutional rights of the American citizen and ravage the operations of major criminals.

As I departed Oklahoma for my next stop, I continued to see large numbers of uniformed patrol on the roadway. Then I thought of my Trooper's admission that, outside of the fifteen men assigned to his division, there were very few other troopers interested in this line of work. Of the handful that were interested, they were not fully trained or assigned to consistently conduct criminal interception.

While I continued my route north-east, I imagined the potential of the patrolmen and the benefit to the citizens (both in their safety and public finance) if the majority of these "uniforms" were trained and directed in this imperative cause: aggressive contraband and illicit fund detection. With their existing assets dedicated to this ultimate cause, Oklahoma would truly be (to quote the state's preparedness motto) "red dirt ready."

FORFEITURE

On the topic of ethics and principles, what is this talk of taking money from the drug organizations and parlaying the cash to public benefit? The aforementioned Robinhood-like approach seems counter-intuitive. But seizing money from the billionaire cartels and giving to the struggling local governments is lawful and tactful.

This is a war and we need to employ war-like tactics. We know the primary enemy and we should act as all military operations, and seek to cut off the head of the proverbial cobra. That "head" being money: the entire purpose of this evil industry.

As noted before, many local drug enforcement units concentrate on the street dealers, the crack houses, and the teens selling weed in the high schools. While all of these are valid concerns, there are far too many for our less-than-5% local drug units to chase.

The same arteries employed for the contraband influx are the same that are piped for the return of the almighty dollar. The profiles used by drug traffickers are all identifiable and detectable, as are the indicators of a money launderer.

The wisdom of these detection skills has been taught to a very select few local law enforcement officers, whose agencies support the cause of trafficking interdiction. The remainder of local, county, and state law enforcement that elect not to concentrate on the source of the problem prefer to allocate their efforts on thousands of man hours (your tax dollars) per year, to chase the end of the drug food chain with very little return on this investment.

Meanwhile, these agencies who invest in the practice of trafficking detection seize not only tremendous quantities of illicit drugs but also the tremendous quantities of currency sent back through the same identifiable, detectable means as the drugs. As a prime example, the one January week reported into Desert Snow (from the "Dollars" chapter) proving the ability of earning hundreds-of-thousands (occasionally millions) of dollars in cash being smuggled back to the dope suppliers.

Every state in the Union has developed a money laundering-related statute that allows for the seizure of this cash. A typical cash seizure is filed as a civil litigation, i.e. the State of Arizona vs. $1,500,000. A civil court hearing is held between the seizing entity and the holder of the currency. If the currency possessor is bold enough to show up and claim the money (facing some very tough answers from the IRS in return), then the counsel for the seizing entity has the burden to show beyond a reasonable doubt (51% probability) that the currency was used for, or was a result of, nefarious activity.

If successful in their testimony, the seizing agency is awarded the currency for use guided under their state's specific act. Illinois' money laundering act, for example, allows the money to be used for the "*enforcing of laws.*" This broad-based definition could reasonably apply to just about anything under a *law enforcement* agency's roof.

The numbers of local law enforcement's contact with drug-law violators against the numbers of federal law enforcement's (i.e. Illinois' 112,368 to 966) are indicative of the reason for the great discrepancy: constant presence.

Local, county, and state law enforcement are always on duty, 24/7/365. Federal law enforcement is typically responsive to investigative information provided by these local lawmen or confidential sources. They are not on the street, responding to police calls, stopping suspicious vehicles, or conducting general traffic enforcement.

The local law enforcement officer is in the best and primary location to initiate these seizures. Imagine if any given agency began training all of their officers, not just "drug enforcement" officers, with the profiles of international trafficking.

The dent on the influx of illegal drugs that so negatively affect our crime rates would substantially increase, and the seizure of the massive amounts of currency on the outflow could begin to self-fund our law enforcement agencies.

Based on ethical codes, an agency and its affiliated city, county or state entity would not be able to budget dependant on the income from anticipated seized currency. The federal asset forfeiture act specifically speaks against the money-making aspect of forfeiture by stating, "the primary goal of asset forfeiture is to deter criminal activity."

However, money interdiction is criminal interdiction. Cash is the sole driving force behind their activity. Nothing is more hampering to a criminal organization than intercepting their currency. It upsets their entire process of product out, profit in. Imagine the correlation to a legitimate cash-based business if most of their bank drops were robbed while en route to the deposit: crippling.

Like the potential demonstrated by those very few patrolmen, consider the local effect of seizing millions of dollars of a cartel bank drop.

Corridor F, Section C: Missouri

"A superior man is modest in speech, but superior in his actions."

-Confucius

Central Missouri has a rich history as a western gateway, with true "country" appeal. Cut between the rolling Ozark Mountains, the region is host to a relaxed and peaceful way of life. Far from urban sprawls and complexities, its people seem to live by tradition and simplicity.

I landed at a Sheriff's Department, serving a relatively small populated county of less than 50,000. The median household income for the area is less than $38,000. County Sheriff's Offices in surrounding jurisdictions have dangerously low budgets and minimal assets. Even their patrol cars are known to break down on the way to an emergency call.

The particular agency that I found boasted a large office, a state-of-the-art training facility, high-end equipment and full uniforms provided for their deputies, and a car fleet that resembled a Chrysler new car lot. All of these royalties were the result of the work of one man.

Before I met him face-to-face, I knew he had seventeen years of criminal patrol experience, placing him in the Robbie Bishop/Mike Lewis era. His seizure history was nationally renowned, taking a whopping thirty-seven pounds of the extremely deadly narcotic-heroin-off the streets during a single stop and dismantling several international drug organizations in one fell swoop during other encounters. To say the least, I had images of a man of great stature and fortitude.

While I gazed out the window of the office lobby at the mass of fancy squad cars, I heard a quick, mild pitched, New York-accented voice call my first name.

I turned to see a stocky little Sicilian man with a uniform that resembled that of a janitor, more than a police professional, holding the door for me. He was a fast talker and a spastic mover, with self-admitted attention deficit disorder. This became more and more evident as we sat along a roadway in his county and I watched him jump side to side in his seat to calm his nerves.

But this was the way the man operated, and operate he does. Averaging $2.5 million per year in cash seizures, alone, the deputy allows his agency to flourish in a region that otherwise suffers from poorly funded government services. The Sheriff in this county (who also has ten years of criminal interception experience while he was a Trooper with the Highway Patrol) has done a tremendous service to his community by dedicating his deputy, full-time, to this cause.

As we sat in his patrol car, he told me stories highlighting his dedication. He explained that he has seen the undeniable outcome of single encounter drug seizures made on his superficially insignificant stretch of highway turning to dramatic criminal interceptions that had cross-country aftershocks, and led to abundant wealth for his county.

While he receives constant accolades from his co-workers and supervisors, he believes that everyone in the agency has a job to do, and this assignment is his. He tries to remain as anonymous in his work as I make him in my writing. But he also sees it as the singularly most important activity in law enforcement, an opinion that he demonstrates on a constant basis.

To capture this man's dedication and determination after seventeen years is a daunting task. He defines his passion for vigilance of the roadways that dissect his county by recalling days of missing meals, spending off-duty time on patrol, and urinating in empty water bottles so he did not have to take a bathroom break from his perch.

As he stopped and spoke with motorists for varying traffic violations, his approach was relaxed and inviting. It was as if he had met an old friend and they were catching up on past-times during each detention. Even after a few prying questions and the occasional consensual glance over of the car's interior, the occupants would thank *him* as they were released from the side of the road. It was as if he had a hypnotic effect on the motorist, and his mere gentility positively directed the course of the short relationship.

When I pointed this uniqueness out to him, he acknowledged that police owe everyone equal respect and, while we criminal patrollers try to provide a service of the upmost vitality, respect from people in return is what allows us to thrive. He then cited an encounter with a gentleman who was trafficking twenty kilos of cocaine across the country until this Missouri deputy pulled him to the shoulder of the highway.

After talking this major criminal into a pair of handcuffs, the man told the deputy that he had a handgun in his underwear and was contemplating killing him. The only thing that saved this deputy that day was his demeanor. The potentially violent offender told the deputy he did not shoot him because he was simply just "too nice."

The deputy's career is nearing the limits of minimum service time, but based on his drive and desire, his county can hope to have him for another twenty years. But what if his county trained two more men to conduct the same patrols during the other sixteen hours of the day? Could they potentially triple their income? Could they return an equal amount from their tax-based budget to the county's general fund, in turn, enhancing or initiating an even broader base of vital government services to all of the citizens?

The answers to these questions are at the disposal of the administrators, but the potential is proven by seventeen years of outstanding productivity. The potential is limitless.

DANGEROUS SURRENDER

"History does not long entrust the care of freedom to the weak or the timid."

-Dwight D. Eisenhower

Within this decade, we have seen a number of states legalize cannabis in some fashion. The entire country of Mexico decriminalized possession of small amounts of cocaine, heroin, and marijuana, while remaining the pipeline for an estimated 80% of the drugs that flow into our country. We have heard a number of local, county and state authorities acknowledge that the war on drugs is most likely lost and it is time to focus on a new crime strategy.

In a January, 2010 Christian Science Monitor article, the Baltimore, Maryland Police Chief is highlighted for his campaign against guns, not drugs, in his notoriously violent city. Even the citizens refer to their hometown as Bloodymore, Murderland. The Chief explains that citizens "understand" drugs, but they do not understand or tolerate the gun carriers.[xix]

Typically in modern crimes, guns are merely an accoutrement to the drug trade.

Why do thugs carry guns on the corner?

To protect and defend their drug territory.

Why do criminals rob people and businesses at gun point?

To obtain money for drugs.

Why do people get shot during suspicious back alley meetings?

Drug deals gone bad.

What are 87% of arrestees for violent crimes under the influence of, during the commission?

DRUGS.

To allow narcotic enforcement to take a back seat to any other crime opens Pandora's Box.

The article shifted to the author's ride-along with the Chief, during which he turned over three young men caught smoking marijuana to their mother, instead of locking them up.

In that, I agree. The young men inhaling cannabis on the corner is not our target in the "war." Even the crack dealers and the guy with the "kilo" (who the Chief describes busting while serving as a narcotics agent) are almost irrelevant.

It is the overt, identifiable, profile-able, and detectable drug traffickers arduously working our highways, bi-ways, freight systems, and airways with metric ton quantities[xx] of deadly narcotics that are our targets.

In continuum of our battle's collapse, we have seen the abolishment of the most dependable and judiciously-recognized asset in contraband and currency detection: drug sniffing canines. Local public services have been reduced due to government budget tightening from their dependency on tax dollars, that are no longer streaming in based on the ailing economy.

In line with this degradation, police agencies look to trim supplemental divisions within their agency to avoid "waste." Mistakenly, police canine teams are categorized as a drain on funds by many entities.

The singularly most effective tool (supported by a bulk of criminal and civil case law) for the ethical seizure of laundered currency and drugs has been cast aside as a non-essential unit by police departments who fail to direct this asset in the right direction. While some local police agencies seize money by the suitcase-load with their detector dogs at the lead; others do not train, direct or support this asset to its full potential.

In one rural county in Oklahoma, a police canine team, whose Sheriff's Office dedicates their full-time service to monitoring the main thoroughfare for trafficking activity, draws an annual average of $400,000 in cash and assets (typically cars and trucks forfeited by traffickers)[xxi]. The seized and subsequently forfeited funds are used to purchase new police vehicles, gasoline for daily patrols, and miscellaneous equipment needs.

These costs would typically be an expense to the citizens of this county, but based on the administration's devotion to this cause, the office is able to support a portion of their services based on the directed hard work of their deputies.

A neighboring county sheriff's office directly to their west (sharing the same thoroughfare and demographics) recently phased out their detection canine team and struggles with the same budget crisis that many other agencies face when relying solely on tax-based funding. An unnecessary suffering.

The working solution is clear. In the Oklahoma example, it is often right next door, but still unseen. This is a war, not skeet shooting. In war you seek to inflict the most damage possible with each strike. It is guided missiles and "shock and awe." Not errant sprays from a shotgun at small random targets. It is directed and supported training and pro-activity that will win the battle. Not responsive, undirected, unsupplemented services.

Hundreds of local law enforcement agencies have proven the outstanding results of this brand of drug detection, but by-in-large, we continue to dedicate only five percent of our police to fight our most crucial battle. Three of that five percent are trained and assigned to detect these major criminals. Of the over 680,000 uniformed police working the streets of our nation, less than 40,000 of them are provided with the resources and information that is required to intercept interstate trafficking.

And we wonder why there has never been any substantial progress made in the "war."

Corridor F, Section D: Illinois

"Always bear in mind that your own resolution to success is more important than any other one thing"

-Abraham Lincoln

While passing through the metropolis of St Louis, I realized that I had not seen a single uniformed patrol presence monitoring the highways of Missouri since I left my Sicilian friend. And before him, I had only seen one patrolman working an accident scene since I left Oklahoma. As I pulled into my final stop in a small town (25,000 population) in southwestern Illinois, I knew there was little to no drag net on the remainder of the route northeast into Chicago.

Besides a few state troopers who took it upon themselves to occasionally seek out narco-traffickers, once the drugs crossed the Illinois border it would be up to the piece-meal reactionary drug investigation units, in and around the big city, to track down small bits of the bulk shipments after they arrived and were distributed. This tour clarified why law enforcement only netted 1% of the illicit drugs that flow into our country and why we, as a nation, were so handily losing the "war on drugs".

It is the basic fact that we, as a nation, consistently fail to direct our resources on the interception of drug shipments that pass under our noses on a daily basis.

This town just east of the official "gateway to the west" was one of the last of our country's defenses for the interception of deadly narcotics traveling into the eastern region of the United States. The village police agency began including narcotic trafficker interception techniques in the mid-1990's as part of its normal patrol duties and they quickly manifested tremendous drug and money seizures. Shortly after the inception, they began dedicating more and more time and resources to this cause, bringing parallel results.

Despite the significant success, the city board began balking at the use of their officers to solve the nation's drug problem, and argued that their police resources should be used to patrol their side streets and not the major thoroughfares. A new police administration in town buckled under the pressure and surrendered to conducting this specific enforcement activity only on a part-time basis as an overtime detail (with the payroll for this additional assignment being paid by money seized from previous campaigns).

The town's retroactive and counter-intuitive policy made me hesitant to visit this agency. However, the results that their dedicated officers were attaining on a very part-time basis, despite the unsupportive atmosphere, deserved some attention. Also, this functioning dichotomy was an excellent example of America's administrative ignorance (by marjoram) to a cause that proves itself, pays for itself, and potentially saves us all.

In just a few short months in 2009, the officers had already seized over $2 million in cash alone. With approximately 80% of that amount being returned to the police for use under a broad umbrella, it seemed the city board would applaud and welcome the fruits of their labor and capitalize on the wealth. Unfortunately, the program was still considered the black swan of the police department and the few officers who participated in it were growing understandably frustrated.

I climbed into a squad car with a patrolman who trained and worked in this facet of patrol since its beginning in the town. To this date, his continued accomplishments make a damaging impact on the illegal drug trade across the country. And while his employer's dismissive outlook on the importance of his work put a damper on his spirit, it does not derail his dedication.

He had traveled the nation, working with local and federal law enforcement agencies, concluding large scale investigations that he had initiated with one casual street encounter in his village. Other officers from his agency had similar successes and this obscure faction of patrol officers understand this brand of work is the most important task local law enforcement can undertake.

His commitment to this cause was immediately apparent in his work ethic, as we dashed out early in the morning to a commercial parcel hub in town to examine the day's incoming load. While standing along the busily working package pickers, he quickly and discreetly grabbed a suspicious box commingled amongst the others. His instincts were dead-on as his agency's drug sniffing dog mauled the box with excitement.

After acquiring a search warrant for the package, we learned it contained illicit narcotics destined for a nearby university. After turning over the box to a local drug detective for the follow-up investigation, he anxiously hit the main thoroughfare, focused on rooting out a smuggler.

As I had seen along the road in the last three states, this officer's professionalism and respect for the public and their constitutional rights were above reproach. Having learned from the same specific schools as the other present-day interceptors, he was able to discern the legitimacy of a person with little, to no, invasiveness. Within a few short hours of patrol we netted a motorist meeting a few alerting criteria. And within a few short minutes of the encounter, he turned to me with a thumbs-up and said "we got one."

It was bittersweet to me. I had contemplated the justification of not seeing any seizures during my trip as a realization that this cause requires constant vigilance and relentless pursuit. Based on the agencies' histories, even if I had not seen a seizure, their long-term statistics spoke for themselves. However, it was rewarding to see this level of dedication and persistence pay off, as the officer cut open one of the car's tires and removed bundles of drugs headed for the Great Lakes region.

As he pointed his pistol at the driver of the vehicle, and ordered him to the ground, it was quite surreal for me. Being a sworn police officer, now back in the state I am sworn to protect, and a fellow officer was actively taking down a major criminal that "we" intercepted. I found myself (uncharacteristically) glancing from the pile of drugs, to the car it came from, to the bad guy laying himself face-down on the hard ground, and thinking: "cool, four days, four states, it all paid off."

Rest assured, I eventually switched out from my day-dream and put hands on the smuggler, securing him with a set of handcuffs I had tucked into my jacket on the first day of the trip. As I helped the man back to his feet and into an awaiting squad car, my host returned to the suspect's vehicle where he began pulling bundle after bundle out of the tire. I could see the suspect's gut sinking as I looked into his eyes. I could also see the sense of pride and accomplishment brimming in the interdictor's eyes.

By the time we returned to the Police Department, the smuggler had already decided to join forces with the arresting officer and arranged to complete the delivery. After another twelve hours of work, to include a trip to northern Indiana, more arrests were made and, of course, more drug money was seized.

Witnessing the work of those police agencies in such a short amount of time was a lot to digest. Each entity had its own brand and style, some drastically different than others, some even arguing practices of the next. But despite their differences, each interdictor was as focused and intent on the same cause as the other.

Observing the varying personalities was as much a treat as it was to soak up their information and perseverance. This awkward brotherhood is on the threshold of creating a major shift in the manner in which local government and law enforcement conduct their business, much to their credit and much to the benefit of our nation.

Idealism Meets Practical Application

"Service to country and self-sacrifice often go unnoticed and unappreciated by the undeserving, however notable the deed. But among men with principle and honor, principle, and honor are enough."

-Herodotus

Interdiction operations are well established in police departments large and small across the country, and their results are astounding.

In scattered locations throughout our country, the direct attack on smugglers continues on a daily basis. For the sake of ensuring that their successes continue to sky rocket, it is important that the names and locations of these agencies remain anonymous. However, I will paint a general geographic picture of a few more agencies that are working tirelessly to turn the tide.

In a quiet, unassuming county in South Carolina, the local Sheriff's Department has taken it upon themselves to key in on the activities of drug traffickers as a method to not only deter criminal activity, but also to generate substantial revenue for law enforcement. The county, itself, is of moderate size with a total population of just over 280,000.

Typical county Sheriff's departments in this demographic (like others cited before), who are required to provide jails, civil services, and criminal warrant maintenance, as well as police patrols, are solely funded by tax dollars. Their services are usually the bare minimum and the training their officers are provided leaves much to be desired. The equipment they deploy on the streets on a daily basis is often dangerously outdated and ineffective.

However, this agency places itself in a position to thrive on the fruits of the drug-runner's labor. While they dedicate several deputies to concentrate on these efforts full-time, they also operate occasional criminal interdiction campaigns on their thoroughfares to root out traffickers in mass.

During one recent campaign, one of the first encounters netted a man driving with $2.5 million cash, in drug money. This stop, alone, would have been enough to augment the Sheriff's budget and provide state-of-the-art vehicles and equipment for at least a year. But the one week campaign did not end there. By the end of this particular emphasis, the Sheriff's Department had $8 million cash in the bank.

Other municipalities and county government agencies across America dedicate at least a portion of their policing resources to interdicting the flow of drugs and money at the point of entry or exit. Another small police department in southern Illinois allows one or two officers to work the main thoroughfare to detect traffickers.

In just one six month period (that the agency's administration described as being abnormally "slow") officers conducting this type of patrol detained just over $2 million in cash, 10 kilograms of cocaine, and 300 lbs of marijuana. For a small, 45 man police department in a quiet community, the seizure of this type of cash results in dramatically expanded service capability for the town it serves.

Additionally, when this small village's policemen seize drugs passing onto other parts of the country, they typically pass the information on to the agency where the drugs were destined. This networking results in additional asset forfeiture income from seizures made during follow up investigation at the destination point. Therefore, the officers have not only made a strong impact in the international war on drugs, but they've also accrued additional, tangible income to support municipal services in their hometown.

With the millions of dollars of unexpected income per year, the agency purchased high-end equipment, to include assault rifles to protect their officers and defend their citizens. The city also built a technologically advanced 9-1-1 dispatch center and hired three community service officers, who conduct numerous daily duties to enhance the quality of life for the town's residents.

This village police agency is one of many entities who continue to face scrutiny from the people they serve. Wondering if the time spent on ferreting out these passer-throughs is relevant to their well-being.

It is vital for them, and for us all, to understand that the effort of these officers interdicting drugs passing on to other parts of the state or nation directly affects the quality of life in your community. Once it passes through your town, the shipments arrive at a distribution point, where it is broken down, and sent back out. Realistically, a portion of that load will land on your soil. Not to mention, chances are that as the drugs pass through, the traffickers are stopping in the area and using your hotels or restaurants to conduct the money or drug transfers that would yield the associated increase in crime.

So how does this affect you? If you were a business with employees who are trained and dedicated to draw your entity millions of extra dollars per year, would you direct them to continue with other, unassociated duties? Or would you direct their constant attention on capitalization? Our civil service employees are already in place. The capitalization is within our reach.

"87%, $18 TO $39 BILLION, 1%..."

"Let every nation know, whether it wishes us well or ill, that we shall pay any price, bear any burden, meet any hardship, support any friend, oppose any foe to assure the survival and the success of liberty."

- John F. Kennedy

The Center for Disease Control published a report in 2009 showing that from 1999 to 2006, the number of poisoning-related deaths almost doubled from 20,000 to 37,000. In 2006, 90% of those deaths involved illicit narcotics[xxii]. I have known people, personally and professionally, who have been killed by drug overdose. I have seen the struggle of a mother and father-whose child committed petty crimes against them and society to abscond enough money for their next injection. I have seen the hopeless pain in their eyes when they found their son or daughter blue and cold on the floor with a needle in their arm.

Regardless of the statistic you throw at the issue, the primary source of crime in America is plain, clear, and identifiable. The course of action to overcome the influx of narcotics has been scripted and proven by pioneers in local law enforcement. Less than three percent of our nation's police officers have been trained and directed in the specific detection of bulk narcotic shipments flowing into or through our communities. The uniformed patrol officer is the most overt and constant presence in law enforcement, making them the tip of our nation's spear in the "war."

Known as our "thin blue line," they are also the last line of defense. Whether it is international terrorism or the destructive methods of drug smugglers, uniformed police are readily in place, 24 hours a day, 7 days a week to detect this activity. The only requirement to unlocking this potential is training and direction.

Strategically speaking, the inability to comprehend the scope of a problem dramatically impacts the correction of a problem. In the case of our "war on drugs," the interdiction pioneers and organizations like the National Criminal Enforcement Association and Desert Snow have expanded our comprehension to unprecedented levels. We know where and how the drugs enter our communities; we know where and how our currency flows out to the cartels. We know these drug trafficking organizations are responsible for this invasion on our well-being, freedom, and self-guiding independence; our autonomy. We know how the dope comes in and we know how the cash goes out . . . it is our mission to halt it.

By arming our men and women in blue with the knowledge of trafficking techniques and profiles, and assigning them to focus attention on primary thoroughfares and parcel points by which these shipments arrive and pass, we can and will achieve substantial victories. Thereby, placing our nation far from our position of surrender and inundation where we currently stagnate.

Local drug enforcement units and federal drug enforcement agencies struggle to keep up with the constant volley of narcotics entering our country. Our local police patrols are the missing link that emboldens the shield against dangerous drugs landing in our communities.

As I open my local newspaper, I read about 120 pink slips going out to teachers in my children's school district. I listen to the local politicians talk about furloughing or laying-off police or firefighters to make ends meet. I hear the radio and television media preparing us for tax hikes against our already strapped wallets.

Then I see the victories of a small handful of police agencies that plug their patrolmen into these interception schools and pull in expendable cash hand over fist: $8 million during a one week campaign, $2 million in just six months for a small town conducting part time interception-specific activities, and over $427 million dollars in just five years of seizures posted by less than 3% of law enforcement trained by just one organization (Desert Snow/Black Asphalt).

Drug money is stolen directly from our hard-working citizens. It is the currency that results from the theft of your identity or the burglary to your car, or the mugging of your daughter or robbing of your local bank, or the theft from your local store that inflates the bill of your next grocery trip, your insurance, and your taxes to pay for law enforcement to respond to a crime that could have been prevented by the interdiction of the drug supply before it even arrived on your street corner.

By educating our men and women in blue with ethical information and tactics, the financial opportunities for local government are endless. Forfeiture of drug proceeds is the essence of law enforcement since cash is the entire driving force behind the drug trade.

The application of the seized cash awarded to law enforcement is generally at the discretion of police administrators. While some take a more conservative approach in interpreting the forfeited currency usage laws, others use it liberally, annually saving their tax payers hundreds of thousands of dollars by self-supporting a percentage of the services they provide.

I have heard many police administrators argue, "it's not that easy. I don't have the manpower. I don't have the resources. It's not our priority."

In response, it *is* essentially "that easy." Our forefathers, and tens-of-thousands of police officers in their wake, have shown this to be an effective means of eradicating massive amounts of illicit drugs from our streets and collecting millions of dollars in narco-proceeds.

If you have police officers, you have the manpower. The constant, overt presence of our uniformed men and women has proven to be one of the most vital, if not *THE* most crucial tactic in drug detection.

Which choice better protects a community: promote your officers to step out and turn on their radar guns in search of the speeding soccer mom-*or* train them, and turn them loose on the chief source of everything they are put in place to fight against?

The standards of the American Red Cross demand that "first responders," such as local police officers, be certified in Cardio Pulmonary Resuscitation (CPR) on an annual basis, based on the likelihood that he or she will be called to the scene of an emergency that will require the initiation of this live-saving procedure. Similar guidelines are in place for annual refresher training on Hazardous Material response, again, due to the uniformed patroller's prevalence and probability of exposure after responding to a call involving a noxious substance.

But for the driving factor behind 87% of people committing crimes in our hometowns on a daily basis, there is no such structured and mandated training or refreshing. For the creator of the majority of calls a police officer responds to, there is no widely-available, government-based and subsidized, mainstream source for up to the minute trafficking intelligence. And for the substance that presses its pushers and users to commit murderous acts (even against innocent citizens and the police) there is no direct, constant, administrative-driven focus for all members of a law enforcement agency to train, plan, and attack.

Sheriff Mike Lewis has trained and directed all of his patrol officers on the art of drug and drug money interdiction. The result has rendered the self-sufficient financial success that I have claimed in my writing. While positioned in a relatively obscure part of our nation, Sheriff Lewis' agency averages annual cash seizures hovering around $250,000.

The Sheriff dedicates the perpetual cash flow to new police cruisers, mobile data terminals (squad car computers), speed radar units, tasers (to reduce liability, save lives, and diminish injury to the patrol officers), stop sticks (made to puncture tires and end car chases), shotguns, rifles, gun racks, new filing systems within his office, and renovation and restoration of a Mobile Command & Communications Center. All of these necessary items are traditionally purchased from tax-payer based general funding. By his dedication to this proven cause, Sheriff Lewis has liberated tax dollars for use in other facets of local government or returned it to the people by way of tax reduction.

Based on Mike Lewis' track record, alone, every community, large or small, obscure or urban, owes it to themselves to make an assessment of their environment and train at least a few of their patrolmen in this skill-set. It is irrelevant what part of the country you are in. If you have a "main street," then you have national-level smuggling occurring under your nose. Quite simply; train your resources, reap the benefits.

During the long course of interviewing and information gathering for this book, I burned a few bridges and damaged a few friendships. For thinking out of the box, per say, and preaching these statistics and proven work ethics to others who have yet to accept them, I've been told such things as I am "out of line," "pissing into the wind," and "crazy" for ever thinking we could change the course of the "war on drugs."

However, I see myself only as a conduit for spreading the message of a trend that has been ignored for far too long. This is not about personal relationships or offending people in high positions; this is about our country, our future and our children. Perhaps I have stepped on a few toes and pressed a few buttons by asking some difficult questions, but it is well worthwhile if the statistics and information presented, herein, changes the course of just one community for the better.

Such is the confrontation we all face in the national progress against narco-terrorism. In America's current political climate, we have seen a refreshing involvement in government from citizens on all levels. Regardless of your position, chances are you have been incited to speak out in some way or another. Perhaps you have been prompted to attend a city council meeting or a village hall gathering coordinated by the federal government, where you shared or at least listened to view points that would effect change.

At the very least, maybe you posted something on your social networking page, declaring a dedication to a certain political direction. This sort of action, any sort of action, is needed to encourage our local government to explore these revenue and crime-fighting breakthroughs.

To the citizen: it is your position to ask your local law enforcement provider if they are doing all that they can in this regard to combat crime on a local and national level. As a police officer, no other cause exemplifies what we raised our right hand, and swore to and signed on the dotted line for than the fight against drug influx. And to the local government leader, it is your obligation to explore every revenue option to augment your tax payers input. It is imperative that your law enforcement agency dedicate at least a portion of its resources to the well-established tactics of drug and drug-money interception to completely and effectively service your community.

Imagine the potential of your local police positioning themselves to be self-supportive (for at least a portion of their budget). If the police department in a city such as the earlier-cited Aurora, Illinois anchors just three to four million dollars per year in outbound drug money (the estimated sum of just four weeks of their current outflow), the return of an equal amount from the police tax-provided budget to the community's general fund would remedy their publicized 2010 deficit of approximately three million dollars. The same deficit that has resulted in lay-offs, vital community program cuts, and a reduction in crucial city services could be resolved by a simple dedication of existing assets to concentrate on a proven government money-maker and crime-stopper.

Asset appropriations like this are occurring in small factions across the country. But for cities such as Aurora who face substantial issues, both criminal and financial, the governing bodies fail to invest in this abundantly available resource. If your local government has yet to research and dedicate at least a portion of their personnel to this cause, ask them why. Contact your police chief, sheriff, alderman, mayor. It is your position and your right to tell them it is time to do their part in cutting-edge revenue generation that may strongly supplement their tax-supported operations.

Perhaps more importantly, interventions like Charlie Hanger's in Oklahoma and contacts like Joe Catalano's in Maryland, as well as the over 30 intercepted terrorists nabbed by Desert Snow-trained operators is the evidence we need to show that this policing method is the answer to our nation's security.

The ability to end the desire to create laws that violate the rights of our citizens in search of illegal immigrants may also be found in these tactics. By increasing our patrols' knowledge of major criminal operations and the detection of their activity, we can not only capture the primary cause of crime in our society (illicit drugs and the multitude of cash that drives their industry) but all forms of national and international threats that routinely challenge our peace and drain our national dollar.

In late 2010, the city of Aurora, Illinois moved to lay off eight police officers in effort to make budgetary ends meet. Within weeks of the decision, perhaps by coincidence or more-likely by strategy, a violent outbreak of gang shootings erupted. One gang member was shot in the head and killed as he stood in his friend's driveway. Two of his associates were also struck by gun fire and survived.

Within the same week, a car occupied by two innocent young women was riddled with bullets blocks away from the first shooting. Days later, an off-duty Aurora police officer was driving down the street in his home town when he saw a scene straight out of a cowboy movie; a gang member wielding a handgun, shooting at another young man running down the sidewalk in front of him.

The off-duty officer recognized the need for his immediate intervention and risked his own life to halt the shooters actions. After drawing his weapon and calling out to the violent gangster, identifying himself as a police officer, the shooter turned and pointed the gun at him. The quick reflexes of the officer resulted in the immediate termination of the criminal. This was a selfless, dutiful and heroic act at a time when his employer was not recognizing the positions of his or his peers as essential.

Government haste, unwillingness to evolve, and an ignorance of the real issues at hand has constantly stagnated or halted law enforcement's acceptance of mass drug and drug money interdiction. Once again, the consideration of proven alternatives could have resulted in the successful budget augmentation needed to retain vital personnel.

Instead of evolving and directing their police to capture some of that aforementioned $720 million annual outflow of narcotic currency to put it to work for their community; corners were cut, jobs were eliminated, violence broke out, and still no real resolution has been found to generate the necessary funds to operate the police department efficiently.

A solid answer to Aurora's and America's war on drugs and crime is at our finger tips. Our forefathers have paved the road and erected the pillars of success. Their disciples continue to prove their cause. The enemies are clear.

The time is now.

i   Incide.com

ii   US Department of Labor, Bureau of Labor Statistics, 2009-2010 graphical data

iii   US Department of Justice

iv   USDOJ/UDBP statiscal averages (www.cbp.gov)

v   2009 Congressional Research Service report

vi   Whitehouse.gov

vii   Center for Disease Control

viii   The Art of War, Sun Tzu

ix   Source: ONDCP 2006 estimates

x   Kane County, IL Sheriff, Aurora, IL Police, USDOJ seizure records

xi   USDOJ/DEA

xii   Cook County Sheriff's/HIDTA '08/'09 annual statistics

xiii   KHPO.com, Tempe, AZ; December 17th, 2009

xiv   www.payscale.com

xv   Desert Snow seizure statistics

xvi   US v. Joaquin Guzman-Loera, 09CR383

xvii   Desert Snow seizure statistics

xviii   Forbes Magazine, 03/11/09 "The World's Billionaires"

xix   Christian Science Monitor, January 2010

xx   Office of National Drug Control Policy

xxi   Canadian County, OK seizure statistics

xxii   Center for Disease Control 2009 annual report

xxiii   2008 ONDCP, ADAM II study

xxiv   Desert Snow Seizure Statistics, January 2010

xxv   DEA History Book, justice.gov

Biography

Charles Haines is employed as a full time Deputy Sheriff in suburban Chicago. He has served as a police officer for 13 years and worked in a narcotics investigation unit for four years of his career. Charles also served as a narcotics detection canine handler for five years. During the last four years, he has seized over 2,000 lbs of cannabis, over nine kilograms of cocaine, over seven kilograms of heroin, over $200,000 in narcotic-related United States Currency, and at least seven vehicles containing aftermarket concealed compartments used for transporting contraband.

Haines has also successfully completed training by the Desert Snow/Black Asphalt Organization in their Phase 1, 2, 3, and 4 Passenger Vehicle and Commercial Motor Vehicle Narcotic Interdiction courses.

Despite not serving in a full time drug interdiction assignment, Charles has intercepted six interstate narcotic traffickers and seized over 290 lbs of cannabis, over seven kilograms of heroin, and over $50,000 in United States currency in 2011, alone.